RESTful Web API Design with Node.js 10
Third Edition

Learn to create robust RESTful web services with Node.js, MongoDB, and Express.js

Valentin Bojinov

D1698383

BIRMINGHAM - MUMBAI

RESTful Web API Design with Node.js 10
Third Edition

Commissioning Editor: Amarabha Banerjee
Acquisition Editor: Reshma Raman
Content Development Editor: Francis Carneiro
Technical Editor: Sachin Sunilkumar
Copy Editor: Shaila Kusanale
Project Coordinator: Sheejal Shah
Proofreader: Safis Editing
Indexer: Mariammal Chettiyar
Graphics: Jason Monteiro
Production Coordinator: Shraddha Falebhai

First published: October 2016
Second edition: October 2017
Third edition: April 2018

Production reference: 1300418

Published by Packt Publishing Ltd.
Livery Place
35 Livery Street
Birmingham
B3 2PB, UK.

ISBN 978-1-78862-332-2

www.packtpub.com

`mapt.io`

Mapt is an online digital library that gives you full access to over 5,000 books and videos, as well as industry leading tools to help you plan your personal development and advance your career. For more information, please visit our website.

Why subscribe?

- Spend less time learning and more time coding with practical eBooks and Videos from over 4,000 industry professionals

- Improve your learning with Skill Plans built especially for you

- Get a free eBook or video every month

- Mapt is fully searchable

- Copy and paste, print, and bookmark content

PacktPub.com

Did you know that Packt offers eBook versions of every book published, with PDF and ePub files available? You can upgrade to the eBook version at `www.PacktPub.com` and as a print book customer, you are entitled to a discount on the eBook copy. Get in touch with us at `service@packtpub.com` for more details.

At `www.PacktPub.com`, you can also read a collection of free technical articles, sign up for a range of free newsletters, and receive exclusive discounts and offers on Packt books and eBooks.

Contributors

About the author

Valentin Bojinov studied computer science at the Technological School of Electronic Systems in Sofia, Bulgaria, a college within the Technical University of Sofia. He holds a B.Sc. in telecommunication and information engineering. Valentin is an expert in Java, SOAP, RESTful web services, and B2B integration. He specializes B2B Integration and Service Oriented Architecture and currently works as an Senior Integration Consultant in an UK consultancy company Estafet Limited.

> *I would like thank my my dad Emil, for encouraging me to study programming almost 20 years ago, and to mummy Anka, for always being there for me! Special thanks to all my mentors from school for showing me how to learn efficiently and to never give up. I also have to mention my extraordinary schoolmates I had the chance to study with!*

About the reviewers

Amit Kothari is a full-stack developer based in Melbourne, Australia. He has more than 12 years experience in designing and developing software systems and has worked on a wide range of projects across various domains including telecommunication, retails, banking and finance.

Amit is also the co-author of the book - *Chatbots for eCommerce: Learn how to build a virtual shopping assistant*.

Erina has completed her master's and proactively working as an assistant professor in the computer science department of Thakur college, Mumbai. Her enthusiasm in web technologies inspires her to contribute for freelance JavaScript projects, especially on Node.js. Her research topics were SDN and IoT, which according to her create amazing solutions for various web technologies when they are used together. Nowadays, she focuses on blockchain and enjoys fiddling with its concepts in JavaScript.

Packt is searching for authors like you

If you're interested in becoming an author for Packt, please visit authors.packtpub.com and apply today. We have worked with thousands of developers and tech professionals, just like you, to help them share their insight with the global tech community. You can make a general application, apply for a specific hot topic that we are recruiting an author for, or submit your own idea.

Table of Contents

Preface

RESTful services have become the de facto standard data feed providers for social services, news feeds, and mobile devices. They deliver a large amount of data to millions of users. Thus, they need to address high-availability requirements, such as reliability and scalability. This book will show you how to utilize the Node.js platform to implement a robust and performant data service. By the end of this book, you will have learned how to implement a real-life RESTful service, taking advantage of the modern NoSQL database to serve both JSON and binary content.

Important topics, such as correct URI structuring and security features, are also covered, with detailed examples, showing you everything you need to know to start implementing the robust RESTful APIs that serve content to your applications.

Who this book is for

This book targets developers who want to enrich their development skills by learning how to develop scalable, server-side, RESTful applications based on the Node.js platform. You also need to be aware of HTTP communication concepts and should have a working knowledge of the JavaScript language. Keep in mind that this is not a book that will teach you how to program in JavaScript. Knowledge of REST will be an added advantage but is definitely not a necessity.

What this book covers

Chapter 1, *REST – What You Did Not Know*, gives you a brief introduction to the history of REST and how it couples with the HTTP protocol.

Chapter 2, *Getting Started with Node.js*, teaches you how to install Node.js and how to work with its package manager to install modules. You'll also develop your first HTTP server application and write automated unit tests for HTTP handler using mock request objects.

Chapter 3, *Building a Typical Web API*, takes you through structuring your application using human-readable URL and URI parameters. You will get to develop a read-only RESTful service application, using the filesystem for storage.

Chapter 4, *Using NoSQL Databases,* showcases how to use the MongoDB NoSQL database, and explains the foundation of document data stores.

Chapter 5, *Restful API Design Guidelines,* explains that there are a number of prerequisites that a RESTful API should meet.

Chapter 6, *Implementing a Full-Fledged RESTful Service,* focuses on implementing a production-ready RESTful service that uses NoSQL to store its data. You will get to learn how to handle binary data and how to version an API while it evolves.

Chapter 7, *Preparing a RESTful API for Production,* explains that feature complete and full-fledged implementations aren't necessarily production-ready.

Chapter 8, *Consuming a RESTful API,* showcases a sample frontend client that serves as a consumption reference implementation.

Chapter 9, *Securing the Application,* covers restricting access to your data by choosing an appropriate authentication approach. You'll then be able to protect data leakage with transport layer security.

To get the most out of this book

1. Inform the reader of the things that they need to know before they start, and spell out what knowledge you are assuming
2. Any additional installation instructions and information they need for getting set up

Download the example code files

You can download the example code files for this book from your account at www.packtpub.com. If you purchased this book elsewhere, you can visit www.packtpub.com/support and register to have the files emailed directly to you.

You can download the code files by following these steps:

1. Log in or register at www.packtpub.com.
2. Select the **SUPPORT** tab.
3. Click on **Code Downloads & Errata**.
4. Enter the name of the book in the **Search** box and follow the onscreen instructions.

Once the file is downloaded, please make sure that you unzip or extract the folder using the latest version of:

- WinRAR/7-Zip for Windows
- Zipeg/iZip/UnRarX for Mac
- 7-Zip/PeaZip for Linux

The code bundle for the book is also hosted on GitHub at `https://github.com/PacktPublishing/RESTful-Web-API-Design-with-Node.js-10-Third-Edition`. In case there's an update to the code, it will be updated on the existing GitHub repository.

We also have other code bundles from our rich catalog of books and videos available at `https://github.com/PacktPublishing/`. Check them out!

Conventions used

In this book, you will find a number of styles of text that distinguish between different kinds of information. Here are some examples of these styles, and an explanation of their meaning.

Code words in text, database tale names, folder names, filenames, file extensions, pathnames, dummy URLs, user input, and Twitter handles are shown as follows: "This tells `npm` that our package depends on the URL and express modules."

A block of code is set as follows:

```
router.get('/v1/item/:itemId', function(request, response, next) {
  console.log(request.url + ' : querying for ' + request.params.itemId);
  catalogV1.findItemById(request.params.itemId, response);
});

router.get('/v1/:categoryId', function(request, response, next) {
  console.log(request.url + ' : querying for ' +
request.params.categoryId);
  catalogV1.findItemsByCategory(request.params.categoryId, response);
});
```

When we wish to draw your attention to a particular part of a code block, the relevant lines or items are set in bold:

```
router.get('/v1/:categoryId', function(request, response, next) {
  console.log(request.url + ' : querying for ' +
request.params.categoryId);
  catalogV1.findItemsByCategory(request.params.categoryId, response);
});
```

Any command-line input or output is written as follows:

```
$ npm install -g express
```

Bold: Indicates a new term, an important word, or words that you see onscreen. For example, words in menus or dialog boxes appear in the text like this. Here is an example:

Warnings or important notes appear like this.

Tips and tricks appear like this.

Get in touch

Feedback from our readers is always welcome.

General feedback: Email feedback@packtpub.com and mention the book title in the subject of your message. If you have questions about any aspect of this book, please email us at questions@packtpub.com.

Errata: Although we have taken every care to ensure the accuracy of our content, mistakes do happen. If you have found a mistake in this book, we would be grateful if you would report this to us. Please visit www.packtpub.com/submit-errata, selecting your book, clicking on the Errata Submission Form link, and entering the details.

Piracy: If you come across any illegal copies of our works in any form on the Internet, we would be grateful if you would provide us with the location address or website name. Please contact us at copyright@packtpub.com with a link to the material.

If you are interested in becoming an author: If there is a topic that you have expertise in and you are interested in either writing or contributing to a book, please visit authors.packtpub.com.

Reviews

Please leave a review. Once you have read and used this book, why not leave a review on the site that you purchased it from? Potential readers can then see and use your unbiased opinion to make purchase decisions, we at Packt can understand what you think about our products, and our authors can see your feedback on their book. Thank you!

For more information about Packt, please visit packtpub.com.

REST – What You Did Not Know

1

Over the last few years, we have started taking for granted that data sources feeding for content, mobile device service feeds, or cloud computing are all driven by modern technologies, such as RESTful web services. Everybody has been talking about how their stateless model allows applications to scale easily and how it emphasizes on clear decoupling between data provisioning and data consumption. Nowadays, architects have started introducing the concept of microservices, aiming to reduce the complexity in systems by splitting their core components into small independent pieces that simply do a single task. So, enterprise-grade software is about to become a composite of such microservices. This makes it easy to maintain, and allows better life cycle management when new parts need to be introduced. Unsurprisingly, most of the microservices are serviced by RESTful frameworks. This fact may leave the impression that REST was invented sometime in the last decade, but that is far from the truth. In fact, REST has been around since the last decade of the previous century!

This chapter will walk you through the foundation of **Representational State Transfer (REST)** and will explain how REST couples with the HTTP protocol. You will look into five key principles that have to be considered while turning any HTTP application into a RESTful service-enabled application. You will also look at the differences between describing RESTful and classic **Simple Object Access Protocol (SOAP)**-based web services. Finally, you will learn how to utilize already-existing infrastructure for your benefit.

In this chapter, we will cover the following topics:

- REST fundamentals
- REST with HTTP
- Essential differences in the description, discovery, and documentation of RESTful services compared to classical SOAP-based services
- Taking advantage of existing infrastructure

REST fundamentals

It actually happened back in 1999, when a request for comments was submitted to the **Internet Engineering Task Force (IETF;** `http://www.ietf.org/`) via RFC 2616: *Hypertext Transfer Protocol-HTTP/1.1*. One of its authors, Roy Fielding, later defined a set of principles built around the HTTP and URI standards. This gave birth to REST as we know it today.

 These definitions were given in `https://www.ics.uci.edu/~fielding/pubs/dissertation/fielding_dissertation.pdf` in the fifth chapter, *Representational State Transfer (REST)*, of Fielding's dissertation called *Architectural Styles and the Design of Network-Based Software Architectures*. The dissertation is still available at `http://www.ics.uci.edu/~fielding/pubs/dissertation/rest_arch_style.htm`.

Let's look at the key principles around the HTTP and URI standards, sticking to which will make your HTTP application a RESTful service-enabled application:

1. Everything is a resource
2. Each resource is identifiable by a **unique identifier (URI)**
3. Resources are manipulated via standard HTTP methods
4. Resources can have multiple representations
5. Communicate with resources in a stateless manner

Principle 1 – Everything is a resource

To understand this principle, one must conceive of the idea of representing data by a specific format and not by a physical file containing a bunch of bytes. Each piece of data available on the internet has a format that describes it, known as the content type; for example, JPEG images, MPEG videos, HTML, XML, text documents, and binary data are all resources with the following content types: image/jpeg, video/mpeg, text/html, text/xml, and application/octet-stream.

Principle 2 – Each resource is identifiable by a unique identifier

Since the internet contains so many different resources, they all should be accessible via URIs and should be identified uniquely. Furthermore, the URIs can be in a human-readable format, despite the fact that their consumers are more likely to be software programs rather than ordinary humans.

Human-readable URIs keep data self-descriptive and ease further development against it. This helps you to keep the risk of logical errors in your programs to a minimum.

Here are a few sample examples of such URIs representing different resources in a catalog application:

- `http://www.mycatalog.com/categories/watches`
- `http://www.mycatalog.com/categories/watches?collection=2018`
- `http://www.mycatalog.com/categories/watches/model-xyz/image`
- `http://www.mycatalog.com/categories/watches/model-xyz/video`
- `http://www.mycatalog.com/archives/2017/categories/watches.zip`

These human-readable URIs expose different types of resources in a straightforward manner. In the preceding example URIs, it is quite clear the data is items in a catalog, which are categorized watches. The first link shows all the items in the category. The second shows only the ones that are part of the 2018 collection. Next is a link pointing to the image of the item, followed by a link to a sample video. The last link points to a resource containing items from the previous collection in a ZIP archive. The media types served per each URI are rather easy to identify, with the assumption that the data format of an item is either JSON or XML, so we can easily map the media type of a self-described URL to one of the following:

- JSON or XML documents describing the items
- Images
- Videos
- Binary archive documents

Principle 3 – Manipulate resources via standard HTTP methods

The native HTTP protocol (RFC 2616) defines eight actions, also known as HTTP verbs:

- GET
- POST
- PUT
- DELETE
- HEAD
- OPTIONS

- TRACE
- CONNECT

The first four of them just feel natural in the context of resources, especially when defining actions for data manipulation. Let's make a parallel with relative SQL databases where the native language for data manipulation is **CRUD** (short for **Create, Read, Update, and Delete**), originating from the different types of SQL statements, INSERT, SELECT, UPDATE, and DELETE, respectively. In the same manner, if you apply the REST principles correctly, the HTTP verbs should be used as shown here:

HTTP verb	Action	HTTP response status code
GET	Retrieves an existing resource.	200 OK if the resource exists, 404 Not Found if it does not exist, and 500 Internal Server Error for other errors.
PUT	Updates a resource. If the resource does not exist, the server can either decide to create it with the provided identifer or return the appropriate status code.	200 OK if successfully updated, 201 Created if a new resource is created, 404 Not found if the resource to be updated does not exist, and 500 Internal Server Error for other unexpected errors.

POST	Creates a resource with an identifier generated at server side or updates a resource with an existing identifier provided from the client. If this verb is to be used only for creating but not for updating, return the appropriate status code.	201 CREATED if a new resource is created, 200 OK if the resource has been updated successfully, 409 Conflict if the resource already exists and update is not allowed, 404 Not Found if the resource to be updated does not exist, and 500 Internal Server Error for other errors.
DELETE	Deletes a resource.	200 OK or 204 No Content if the resource has been deleted successfully, 404 Not Found if the resource to be deleted does not exist, and 500 Internal Server Error for other errors.

Note that a resource might be created by either the POST or PUT HTTP verbs, based on the policy of an application. However, if a resource has to be created under a specific URI with an identifier provided by the client, then PUT is the appropriate action:

```
PUT /categories/watches/model-abc HTTP/1.1
Content-Type: text/xml
Host: www.mycatalog.com

<?xml version="1.0" encoding="utf-8"?>
<Item category="watch">
    <Brand>...</Brand>
    </Price></Price>
</Item>

HTTP/1.1 201 Created
Content-Type: text/xml
Location: http://www.mycatalog.com/categories/watches/model-abc
```

However, in your application, you may want to leave it up to the backend RESTful service to decide where to expose the newly created resource, and thus create it under an appropriate but still unknown or non-existent location.

For instance, in our example, we might want the server to define the identifier of newly created items. In such cases, just use the POST verb to a URL without providing an identifier parameter. Then it is up to the service itself to provide a new unique and valid identifier for the new resource and to expose back this URL via the Location header of the response:

```
POST /categories/watches HTTP/1.1
Content-Type: text/xml
Host: www.mycatalog.com
```

```
<?xml version="1.0" encoding="utf-8"?>
<Item category="watch">
    <Brand>...</Brand>
    </Price></Price>
</Item>

HTTP/1.1 201 Created
Content-Type: text/xml
Location: http://www.mycatalog.com/categories/watches/model-abc
```

Principle 4 – Resources can have multiple representations

A key feature of a resource is that it may be represented in a different format from the one in which it is stored. Thus, it can be requested or created in different representations. As long as the specified format is supported, the REST-enabled endpoint should use it. In the preceding example, we posted an XML representation of a watch item, but if the server had supported the JSON format, the following request would have been valid as well:

```
POST /categories/watches HTTP/1.1
Content-Type: application/json
Host: www.mycatalog.com

{
  "watch": {
    "id": ""watch-abc"",
    "brand": "...",
    "price": {
      "-currency": "EUR",
      "#text": "100"
    }
  }
}
HTTP/1.1 201 Created
Content-Type: application/json
Location: http://mycatalog.com/categories/watches/watch-abc
```

Principle 5 – Communicate with resources in a stateless manner

Resource manipulation operations through HTTP requests should always be considered atomic. All modifications of a resource should be carried out within an HTTP request in an isolated manner. After the request execution, the resource is left in a final state; this implicitly means that partial resource updates are not supported. You should always send the complete state of the resource.

Back to our catalog example, updating the price field of a given item would mean making a PUT request with a complete document (JSON or XML) that contains the entire data, including the updated price field. Posting only the updated price is not stateless, as it implies that the application is aware that the resource has a price field, that is, it knows its state.

Another requirement for your RESTful application to be stateless is that once the service gets deployed on a production environment, it is likely that incoming requests are served by a load balancer, ensuring scalability and high availability. Once exposed via a load balancer, the idea of keeping your application state at server side gets compromised. This doesn't mean that you are not allowed to keep the state of your application. It just means that you should keep it in a RESTful way. For example, keep a part of the state within the URI, or use HTTP headers to provide additional state-related data

The statelessness of your RESTful API isolates the caller against changes at the server side. Thus, the caller is not expected to communicate with the same server in consecutive requests. This allows easy application of changes within the server infrastructure, such as adding or removing nodes.

 Remember that it is your responsibility to keep your RESTful APIs stateless, as the consumers of the APIs would expect them to be.

Now that you know that REST is around 18 years old, a sensible question would be, "Why has it become so popular just quite recently?" Well, we the developers usually reject simple, straightforward approaches and, most of the time, prefer spending more time on turning already-complex solutions into even more complex and sophisticated ones.

Take classical SOAP web services, for example. Their various WS-* specifications are so many, and sometimes so loosely defined, that in order to make different solutions from different vendors interoperable, a separate specification, WS-Basic Profile, has been introduced. It defines extra interoperability rules in order to ensure that all WS-* specifications in SOAP-based web services can work together.

When it comes to transporting binary data with classical web services over HTTP, things get even more complex, as SOAP-based web services provide different ways of transporting binary data. Each way is defined in other sets of specifications, such as **SOAP with Attachment References (SwaRef)** and **Message Transmission Optimization Mechanism (MTOM).** All this complexity was caused mainly because the initial idea of the web service was to execute business logic remotely, not to transport large amounts of data.

The real world has shown us that, when it comes to data transfer, things should not be that complex. This is where REST fits into the big picture—by introducing the concept of resources and a standard means for manipulating them.

The REST goals

Now that we've covered the main REST principles, it is time to dive deeper into what can be achieved when they are followed:

- Separation of the representation and the resource
- Visibility
- Reliability
- Scalability
- Performance

Separation of the representation and the resource

A resource is just a set of information, and as defined by principle 4, it can have multiple representations; however, its state is atomic. It is up to the caller to specify the desired media type with the `Accept` header in the HTTP request, and then it is up to the server application to handle the representation accordingly, returning the appropriate content type of the resource together with a relevant HTTP status code:

- `HTTP 200 OK` in the case of success

- HTTP 400 Bad Request if an unsupported format is given or for any other invalid request information
- HTTP 406 Not Acceptable if an unsupported media type is requested
- HTTP 500 Internal Server Error when something unexpected happens during the request processing

Let's assume that, at server side, we have items resources stored in an XML format. We can have an API that allows a consumer to request the item resources in various formats, such as application/xml, application/json, application/zip, application/octet-stream, and so on.

It would be up to the API itself to load the requested resource, transform it into the requested type (for example, JSON or XML), and either use ZIP to compress it or directly flush it to the HTTP response output.

The caller would make use of the Accept HTTP header to specify the media type of the response they expect. So, if we want to request our item data inserted in the previous section in XML format, the following request should be executed:

```
GET /category/watches/watch-abc HTTP/1.1
Host: my-computer-hostname
Accept: text/xml

HTTP/1.1 200 OK
Content-Type: text/xml
<?xml version="1.0" encoding="utf-8"?>
<Item category="watch">
    <Brand>...</Brand>
    </Price></Price>
</Item>
```

To request the same item in JSON format, the Accept header needs to be set to application/json:

```
GET /categoery/watches/watch-abc HTTP/1.1
Host: my-computer-hostname
Accept: application/json

HTTP/1.1 200 OK
Content-Type: application/json
{
  "watch": {
    "id": ""watch-abc"",
    "brand": "...",
```

```
    "price": {
      "-currency": "EUR",
      "#text": "100"
    }
  }
}
```

Visibility

REST is designed to be visible and simple. Visibility of the service means that every aspect of it should self-descriptive and follow the natural HTTP language according to principles 3, 4, and 5.

Visibility in the context of the outer world would mean that monitoring applications would be interested only in the HTTP communication between the REST service and the caller. Since the requests and responses are stateless and atomic, nothing more is needed to flow the behavior of the application and to understand whether anything has gone wrong.

 Remember that caching reduces the visibility of your RESTful applications and in general should be avoided, unless needed for serving resources subject to large amounts of callers. In such cases, caching may be an option, after carefully evaluating the possible consequences of serving obsolete data.

Reliability

Before talking about reliability, we need to define which HTTP methods are safe and which are idempotent in the REST context. So, let's first define what safe and idempotent methods are:

- An HTTP method is considered to be safe provided that, when requested, it does not modify or cause any side effects on the state of the resource
- An HTTP method is considered to be idempotent if its response stays the same, regardless of the number of times it is requested, am idempotent request always gives back the same request, if repeated identically.

The following table lists which HTTP methods are safe and which are idempotent:

HTTP method	Safe	Idempotent
GET	Yes	Yes
POST	No	No
PUT	No	Yes
DELETE	No	Yes

Consumers should consider operation's safety and the idempotence features in order to be served reliably.

Scalability and performance

So far, we stressed the importance of having stateless behavior for a RESTful web application. The **World Wide Web (WWW)** is an enormous universe, containing huge amount of data and a lot of users, eager to get that data. The evolution of the WWW has brought the requirement that applications should scale easily as their load increases. Scaling applications that have a state is difficult to achieve, especially when zero or close-to-zero operational downtime is expected.

That's why staying stateless is crucial for any application that needs to scale. In the best-case scenario, scaling your application would require you to put another piece of hardware for a load balancer, or bring another instance in your cloud environment. There would be no need for the different nodes to sync between each other, as they should not care about the state at all. Scalability is all about serving all your clients in an acceptable amount of time. Its main idea is to keep your application running and to prevent **Denial of Service (DoS)** caused by a huge amount of incoming requests.

Scalability should not be confused with the performance of an application. Performance is measured by the time needed for a single request to be processed, not by the total number of requests that the application can handle. The asynchronous non-blocking architecture and event-driven design of Node.js make it a logical choice for implementing an application that scales and performs well.

Working with WADL

If you are familiar with SOAP web services, you may have heard of the **Web Service Definition Language (WSDL)**. It is an XML description of the interface of the service and defines an endpoint URL for invocation. It is mandatory for a SOAP web service to be described by such a WSDL definition.

Similar to SOAP web services, RESTful services can also make use of a description language, called WADL. **WADL** stands for **Web Application Definition Language**. Unlike WSDL for SOAP web services, a WADL description of a RESTful service is optional, that is, consuming the service has nothing to do with its description.

Here is a sample part of a WADL file that describes the GET operation of our catalog service:

```xml
<?xml version="1.0" encoding="UTF-8"?>
<application xmlns="http://wadl.dev.java.net/2009/02"
xmlns:service="http://localhost:8080/catalog/"
xmlns:xsd="http://www.w3.org/2001/XMLSchema">
  <grammer>
    <include href="items.xsd" />
    <include href="error.xsd" />
  </grammer>
  <resources base="http://localhost:8080/catalog/categories">
    <resource path="{category}">
      <method name="GET">
        <request>
          <param name="category" type="xsd:string" style="template" />
        </request>
        <response status="200">
          <representation mediaType="application/xml"
element="service:item" />
          <representation mediaType="application/json" />
        </response>
        <response status="404">
          <representation mediaType="application/xml"
element="service:item" />
        </response>
      </method>
    </resource>
  </resources>
</application>
```

This extract of a WADL file shows how application, exposing resources is described. Briefly, each resource must be part of an application. The resource provides a, where it is located with the `base` attribute, and describes each of its supported HTTP methods in a method. Additionally, an optional `doc` element can be used at resource and application to provide additional documentation about the service and its operations.

Though WADL is optional, it significantly reduces the efforts of discovering RESTful services.

Documenting RESTful APIs with Swagger

Public APIs exposed on the web should be well documented, otherwise it would be difficult for developers to use them in their applications. While WADL definitions might be considered a source of documentation, they address a different problem—the discovery of the service. They serve metadata for the services to machines, not to humans. The Swagger project (`https://swagger.io/`) addresses the need for neat documentation of RESTful APIs. It defines a meta description of an API from an almost human-readable JSON format. The following is a sample `swagger.json` file, partially describing the catalog service:

```
{
  "swagger": "2.0",
  "info": {
    "title": "Catalog API Documentation",
    "version": "v1"
  },
  "paths": {
    "/categories/{id}" : {
      "get": {
        "operationId": "getCategoryV1",
        "summary": "Get a specific category ",
        "produces": [
          "application/json"
        ],
        "responses": {
          "200": {
            "description": "200 OK",
            "examples":
              {"application/json": {
                "id": 1,
                "name": "Watches",
                "itemsCount": 550
                }
              }
            }
```

```
        },
        "404": {"description" : "404 Not Found"},
        "500": {"description": "500 Internal Server Error"}
      }
    }
  }
},
"consumes": ["application/json"]
}
```

The `swagger.json` file is really straightforward: it defines a name and version of your API and gives a brief description of each operation it exposes, nicely coupled with a sample payload. But the real benefit from it comes in another subproject of Swagger, called `swagger-ui` (`https://swagger.io/swagger-ui/`), which actually renders this data from `swagger.json` nicely into an interactive web page that only provides documentation, but also allows interaction with the service:

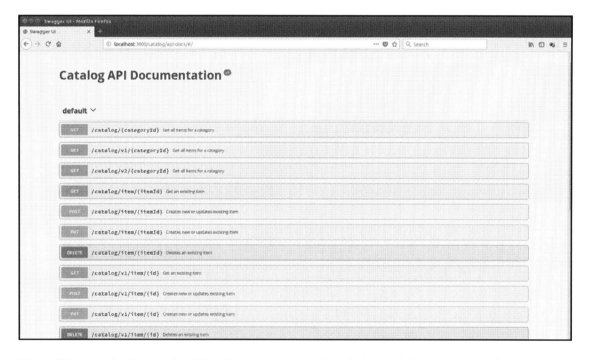

We will have a look at and utilize the `swagger-ui` Node.js module to provide the API that we will develop later in the book, with up-to-date documentation.

Taking advantage of the existing infrastructure

The best part of developing and distributing RESTful applications is that the infrastructure needed is already out there, available to you. As RESTful applications use the existing web space heavily, you need to do nothing more than follow the REST principles when developing. In addition, there are plenty of libraries available out there for any platform, and I do mean any platform. This eases the development of RESTful applications, so you just need to choose your preferred platform and start developing.

Summary

In this chapter, you learned about foundation of a REST, looking at five key principles that transform a web application into a REST-enabled application. We made a brief comparison between RESTful services and classical SOAP web services, and finally took a look at how RESTful services are documented and how we can simplify the discovery of the services we develop.

Now that you know the basics, we are ready to dive into the Node.js way of implementing RESTful services. In the next chapter, you will learn about the essentials of Node.js and the accompanying tools that it is necessary to use and understand in order to build a real-life fully-fledged web service.

Getting Started with Node.js

2

In this chapter, you will gain your first real Node.js experience. We will start by installing Node.js, along with some modules we will use throughout this book. Then, we will set up a development environment. Throughout the book, the Atom IDE will be used. Yes, GitHub's online editor has finally landed for desktop environment and is available on a platform of your preference!

Next, we will create a workspace and start developing our first Node.js application. It will be a simple server application processing incoming HTTP requests. We will go one step further, demonstrating how to modularize and unit test our JavaScript code. Finally, we will deploy our first application on the Heroku Cloud Application platform.

To sum up, in this chapter, we will cover the following topics:

- Installing Node.js
- Installing the Express framework and other modules
- Setting up a development environment
- Handling HTTP requests
- Modularizing code
- Testing Node.js
- Deploying an application

Installing Node.js

Let's start our journey through Node.js with a Node.js installation. Installers are available for both Windows and macOS at `https://nodejs.org/en/download/`. At the time of writing, Node.js 10 has just been released as the current version, and is about to become the next Long Term Support version, in August 2018. Linux users can either build Node.js from the available Linux binaries or make use of their package manager, as Node.js is available with most of the popular package repositories for different Linux distributions. For instance, Ubuntu and other Debian-based distributions should first point to the latest Node.js 10 package and then install via the `apt-get` command from the shell:

```
curl -sL https://deb.nodesource.com/setup_10.x | sudo -E bash -
sudo apt-get install nodejs
```

If you decide to go with an installer available for macOS or Windows, a wizard will guide you through a rather typical installation procedure, where you will have to accept the Node.js license agreement and then provide an installation path.

Linux users performing installations via package managers will need to install **Node Package Manager (npm)** separately; we will do that in the next section.

After a successful installation, you should have Node set on your `PATH` environment variable.

The installer will have preselected for you the Node.js runtime, npm, shortcuts to online documentation resources, as well as the option to add Node.js and npm to your operating system `PATH` environment variable.

To verify that your installation was successful, execute the following from your shell:

```
node --version
```

 At the time of writing, the latest Node.js version is 10.0.0 so, as expected, this version number will be the output of the version check. Node.js 10 will be the next Long Term Supported version, so it will stay actual for the next few years

Npm

Node.js eases support to third-party open source-developed modules by providing **npm**. It allows you, as a developer, to easily install, manage, and even provide your own module packages. The npm package repository is available at `http://www.npmjs.org/` and is accessible via its command-line interface.

If you didn't use the installer, then you will need to install `npm` separately. For example, Ubuntu users can make use of their package installer as follows:

```
apt-get npm install
```

If you upgraded your Node.js installation and you had previously installed npm 5.6, you would be asked to upgrade it to version 6. To do that, just execute:

```
sudo npm i -g npm
```

Once npm is installed, it is useful to set it permanently in your user profile's `PATH` environment variable by editing the `~/.profile` file to export the path to npm as follows:

```
export PATH=$PATH:/path/to/npm
```

After a successful npm installation, use npm's `ls` option to display the currently-installed Node.js modules:

```
bojinov@developer-machine:~$ npm ls
/home/bojinov
├─┬ accepts@1.3.3
│ ├─┬ mime-types@2.1.13
│ │ └── mime-db@1.25.0
│ └── negotiator@0.6.1
├── array-flatten@1.1.1
├─┬ cache-control@1.0.3
│ ├─┬ cache-header@1.0.3
│ │ ├── lodash.isnumber@2.4.1 deduped
│ │ ├── lodash.isstring@2.4.1
│ │ └── regular@0.1.6 deduped
│ ├─┬ fast-url-parser@1.1.3
│ │ └── punycode@1.4.1
│ ├─┬ glob-slasher@1.0.1
│ │ ├── glob-slash@1.0.0
│ │ ├─┬ lodash.isobject@2.4.1
│ │ │ └── lodash._objecttypes@2.4.1
│ │ └─┬ toxic@1.0.0
│ │ └── lodash@2.4.2
│ ├─┬ globject@1.0.1
```

```
|   |   └──── minimatch@2.0.10 extraneous
|   ├──── lodash.isnumber@2.4.1
|   ├──── on-headers@1.0.1
|   └──── regular@0.1.6
├──── content-disposition@0.5.1
├──── content-type@1.0.2
├──── cookie@0.3.1
├──── cookie-signature@1.0.6
```

Installing the Express framework and other modules

Now that we have npm installed, let's make use of it and install some of the modules we will be using heavily throughout this book. The most important among them is the Express framework (http://www.expressjs.com/). It is a flexible web application framework for Node.js, providing a robust RESTful API for developing single or multi-page web applications. The following command will download the Express module from the npm repository and make it available for our local Node.js installation:

```
npm install -g express
```

You will find the express module among the results of an npm ls after a successful installation. Later in this chapter, we will learn how to write unit tests for our Node.js modules. We will need the nodeunit module for that purpose:

```
npm install nodeunit -g
```

The -g option will install nodeunit globally. This means that the module will be stored at a central place on your filesystem; usually, that is either /usr/lib/node_modules or /usr/lib/node, but that can be configured to the global configuration of your Node.js. Globally installed modules are available to all running node applications.

Locally installed modules will be stored in a node_modules subdirectory of the current working directory of your project and will be available only to that single project.

Now, coming back to the nodeunit module—it provides basic assert test functions for creating basic unit tests as well as tools for executing them.

Before starting to develop with Node.js, we have one more thing to look into: the package descriptor file of a Node.js application.

All Node.js applications or modules contain a `package.json` descriptor file. It provides meta-information about the module, its authors, and the dependencies it uses. Let's take a look at the `package.json` file of the `express` module we installed earlier:

```
{
  "_from": "express",
  "_id": "express@4.16.1",
  "_inBundle": false,
  "_integrity": "sha512-
STB7LZ4N0L+81FJHGla2oboUHTk4PaN1RsOkoRh9OSeEKylvF5hwKYVX1xCLFaCT7MD0BNG/gX2
WFMLqY6EMBw==",
  "_location": "/express",
  "_phantomChildren": {},
  "_requested": {
    "type": "tag", "registry": true, "raw": "express", "name": "express",
    "escapedName": "express","rawSpec": "", "saveSpec": null, "fetchSpec":
"latest"
  },
  "_requiredBy": [
    "#USER"
  ],
  "_resolved": "https://registry.npmjs.org/express/-/express-4.16.1.tgz",
  "_shasum": "6b33b560183c9b253b7b62144df33a4654ac9ed0",
  "_spec": "express",
  "_where": "/home/valio/Downloads",
  "author": {
    "name": "TJ Holowaychuk",
    "email": "tj@vision-media.ca"
  },
  "bugs": {
    "url": "https://github.com/expressjs/express/issues"
  },
  "bundleDependencies": false,
  "contributors": [
    {
      "name": "Aaron Heckmann",
      "email": "aaron.heckmann+github@gmail.com"
    },
    ...,
    {
      "name": "Young Jae Sim",
      "email": "hanul@hanul.me"
    }
  ],
```

```
  "dependencies": {
    "accepts": "~1.3.4",
    "array-flatten": "1.1.1",
    "body-parser": "1.18.2",
    ...,
    "type-is": "~1.6.15",
    "utils-merge": "1.0.1",
    "vary": "~1.1.2"
  },
  "deprecated": false,
  "description": "Fast, unopinionated, minimalist web framework",
  "devDependencies": {
    "after": "0.8.2",
    "connect-redis": "~2.4.1",
    ...,
    "should": "13.1.0",
    "supertest": "1.2.0",
    "vhost": "~3.0.2"
  },
  "engines": {
    "node": ">= 0.10.0"
  },
  "files": ["LICENSE", "History.md", "Readme.md", "index.js","lib/"],
  "homepage": "http://expressjs.com/",
  "keywords": [
    "express", "framework", "sinatra", "web", "rest", "restful", "router",
"app", "api"
  ],
  "license": "MIT",
  "name": "express",
  "repository": {
    "type": "git",
    "url": "git+https://github.com/expressjs/express.git"
  },
  "scripts": {
    "lint": "eslint .",
    "test": "mocha --require test/support/env --reporter spec --bail --
check-leaks test/ test/acceptance/"
  },
  "version": "4.16.1"
}
```

The name and the version of the package are mandatory properties for every module. All other pieces of meta-information, such as the contributors list, repository type and location, license information, and so on, are optional. One of the most interesting properties, which is worth mentioning, is the `dependencies` property. It tells npm which modules your package depends on. Let's take a deeper look at how this is specified. Each dependency has a name and a version.

This tells npm that the package depends on the `accepts` module with version 1.3.4 and the `body-parse` module with version 1.8.2. So, when npm installs the module, it will implicitly download and install the latest minor versions of the dependencies, in case they are not already available.

The version of a dependency is specified in the following format: `major.minor.patch-version`. You can specify npm if you want npm to use exactly the specified version, or you can have npm always download the latest available minor version, by starting the version with ~; see the `accepts` dependency for reference.

For more information on versioning, visit the website of the semantic versioning specification at `http://www.semver.org/`.
Depending on automatically managed version may result in backward incompatibility, make sure you test your application each time you switch a version.

Setting up a development environment

JavaScript developers are rarely used to developing their projects in an IDE; most of them use text editors and tend to be prejudiced against anything that contradicts their views. GitHub has finally managed to calm most of them down by releasing the Atom IDE for the desktop environment. This may not solve all of the arguments about which is the best environment, but will at least bring some peace, and let people concentrate on their code, not on the tooling, which in the end is a matter of personal preference. The samples in this book are developed in the Atom IDE, but feel free to use any piece of software that can create files, including command-line editors such as vi or vim, if that would make you feel like a JS superhero, though bear in mind that superheroes are so 20th century!

You can download the Atom IDE from `https://ide.atom.io/`.

It is time to start our first Node.js application, a simple web server responding with `Hello from Node.js`. Select a directory from your project, for example, `hello-node`, then open a shell Terminal from it and execute `npm init`:

```
npm init

package name: (hello-node)
version: (1.0.0)
description: Simple hello world http handler
entry point: (index.js) app.js
test command: test
git repository:
keywords:
author: Valentin Bojinov
license: (ISC)
About to write to /home/valio/nodejs8/hello-node/package.json:

{
  "name": "hello-node",
  "version": "1.0.0",
  "description": "Simple hello world http handler",
  "main": "app.js",
  "scripts": {
    "test": "test"
  },
  "author": "Valentin Bojinov",
  "license": "ISC"
}


Is this ok? (yes) yes
```

A command-line interaction wizard will ask you for your project name, its version, as well as some other metadata such as Git repository, your name, and so on, and will finally preview the `package.json` file it is to generate; when complete, your first Node.js project is ready to begin.

Now is the appropriate time to spend some time on the code convention used in this book; ES6 inline anonymous functions will be used when short callback functions should be defined, while regular javascript function will be used when reusability and testability is expected.

Start the Atom IDE, select **File | Add Project Folder...**, and import the directory you defined the project in. Finally, after a successful import, you will see the generated package.json file in the project. Right-click on the directory, select **New File**, and create a file called hello-node.js:

```
var http = require('http');

http.createServer((request, response) => {
  response.writeHead(200, {
    'Content-Type' : 'text/plain'
  });
  response.end('Hello from Node.JS');
  console.log('Hello handler requested');
}).listen(8180, '127.0.0.1', () => {
  console.log('Started Node.js http server at http://127.0.0.1:8180');
});
```

The hello-node.js file uses the Node.js HTTP module to start listening for incoming requests on port 8180. It will reply with static Hello from Node.JS to each request and will log a hello log entry in the console. Before starting the application, we have to install the http module that creates an HTTP server for it. Let's install it globally together with the --save option, which will add a dependency to it in the package.json file of the project. Then we can start the app:

```
npm install -g http --save
node hello-node.js
```

Opening `http://localhost:8180/` from your browser will result in sending a request to the server application, which will make a log entry in the console and will output `Hello from Node.JS` in your browser:

Handling HTTP requests

Currently, our server application will behave in the same way, no matter what kind of HTTP request is processed. Let's extend it in such a way that it behaves more like an HTTP server, and start differentiating the incoming requests based on their type, by implementing handler functions for each type of request.

Let's create a new `hello-node-http-server.js` as follows:

```
var http = require('http');
var port = 8180;

function handleGetRequest(response) {
  response.writeHead(200, {'Content-Type' : 'text/plain'});
  response.end('Get action was requested');
}

function handlePostRequest(response) {
  response.writeHead(200, {'Content-Type' : 'text/plain'});
  response.end('Post action was requested');
}
```

```
function handlePutRequest(response) {
  response.writeHead(200, {'Content-Type' : 'text/plain'});
  response.end('Put action was requested');
}

function handleDeleteRequest(response) {
  response.writeHead(200, {'Content-Type' : 'text/plain'});
  response.end('Delete action was requested');
}

function handleBadRequest(response) {
  console.log('Unsupported http mehtod');
  response.writeHead(400, {'Content-Type' : 'text/plain'  });
  response.end('Bad request');
}

function handleRequest(request, response) {
  switch (request.method) {
    case 'GET':
      handleGetRequest(response);
      break;
    case 'POST':
      handlePostRequest(response);
      break;
    case 'PUT':
      handlePutRequest(response);
      break;
    case 'DELETE':
      handleDeleteRequest(response);
      break;
    default:
      handleBadRequest(response);
      break;
  }
  console.log('Request processing completed');
}

http.createServer(handleRequest).listen(8180, '127.0.0.1', () => {
  console.log('Started Node.js http server at http://127.0.0.1:8180');
});
```

When we run this application, our HTTP server will recognize the GET, POST, PUT, and DELETE HTTP methods, and will handle them in different functions. To all other HTTP requests, it will gracefully respond with the HTTP 400 BAD REQUEST status code. To interact with the HTTP applications, we will use Postman, available to download from https://www.getpostman.com/. It is a lightweight application for sending HTTP requests to an endpoint, specifying HTTP headers, and providing payload. Give it a try and execute test requests for each of the handler functions we implemented previously:

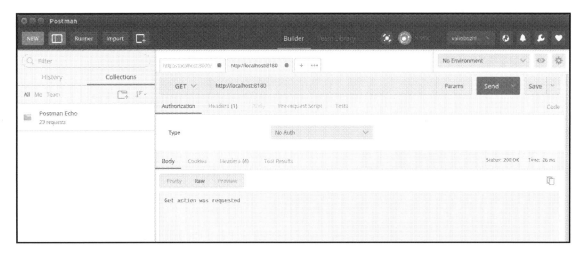

Modularizing code

What we have developed so far is a simple HTTP server application that listens and processes known request types; however, it is not so well structured, as the functions handling the requests are not reusable. Node.js supports modules embracing code isolation and reusability.

 A user-defined module is a logical unit consisting of one or more related functions. The module can export one or more functions to other components while keeping other functions visible only to itself.

We will rework our HTTP server application in such a way that the entire request handling functionality will be wrapped in a module. The module will export only a generic handler function that will take a request object as argument and, based on its request type, it will delegate the handling to inner functions not visible outside the module.

Let's start by creating a new module directory within our project. We will refactor our previous source file by extracting the following functions to a new `http-module.js` file inside the newly created directory:

```javascript
function handleGetRequest(response) {
  response.writeHead(200, {'Content-Type' : 'text/plain'});
  response.end('Get action was requested');
}

function handlePostRequest(response) {
  response.writeHead(200, {'Content-Type' : 'text/plain'});
  response.end('Post action was requested');
}

function handlePutRequest(response) {
  response.writeHead(200, {'Content-Type' : 'text/plain'});
  response.end('Put action was requested');
}

function handleDeleteRequest(response) {
  response.writeHead(200, {'Content-Type' : 'text/plain'});
  response.end('Delete action was requested');
}

function handleBadRequest(response) {
  console.log('Unsupported http mehtod');
  response.writeHead(400, {'Content-Type' : 'text/plain'  });
  response.end('Bad request');
}

exports.handleRequest = function(request, response) {
  switch (request.method) {
    case 'GET':
      handleGetRequest(response);
      break;
    case 'POST':
      handlePostRequest(response);
      break;
    case 'PUT':
      handlePutRequest(response);
      break;
    case 'DELETE':
      handleDeleteRequest(response);
      break;
    default:
      handleBadRequest(response);
      break;
```

```
  }
  console.log('Request processing completed');
}
```

This file creates a user-defined module that exports the `handleRequest` function, making it available to the other components. All the other functions are accessible only within the module. Although the sample exports only one function, a module can export as many functions as is feasible.

Let's use the new `http-module` in the `main.js` file in the `main` directory of our first project. We have to create an `http` server using the Node.js built-in `http` module, and its `createServer` will pass its `handleRequest` function as its argument. It will serve as a callback function that the server will invoke on each request:

```
var http = require('http');
var port = 8180;

var httpModule = require('./modules/http-module');

http.createServer(httpModule.handleRequest).listen(8180, '127.0.0.1', () =>
{
  console.log('Started Node.js http server at http://127.0.0.1:8180');
});
```

We separated the creation of the server socket from the business logic that handles the incoming requests bound to it. The `require` directive is used to import our module. It uses a relative path to it. Try this version as well by executing another test request with the Postman tooling.

 Luckily, we will not be creating our own HTTP handlers when implementing our RESTful-enabled applications. The Express framework will do this for us. The examples in this chapter are meant to provide a clear example of the Node.js possibilities when it comes to handling HTTP requests and how user modules are implemented. We will take a detailed look at the Express framework in `Chapter 3`, *Building a Typical Web API*.

Testing Node.js

Now we will extend our project by providing a unit test for the HTTP module, but before diving into that, let's have a look at how Node.js supports unit testing in general. At the beginning of this chapter, we installed the Nodeunit module. Well, it's about time we started playing around with it.

First, let's create another simple Node.js module that we will use to implement our first unit test. Then we will move to more advanced topics, such as mocking JavaScript objects and using them to create unit tests for our HTTP module.

I have chosen to develop a simple math module that exports functions for adding and subtracting integer numbers, as it is straightforward enough and the results of each operation are strictly defined.

Let's start with the module and create the following `math.js` file in our `module` directory:

```
exports.add = function (x, y) {
  return x + y;
};
exports.subtract = function (x, y) {
  return x - y;
};
```

The next step will be to create a `test-math.js` file in the `test` subdirectory of our project:

```
var math = require('../modules/math');
exports.addTest = function (test) {
  test.equal(math.add(1, 1), 2);
  test.done();
};
exports.subtractTest = function (test) {
  test.equals(math.subtract(4,2), 2);
  test.done();
};
```

Finally, run the test module from a shell Terminal with `nodeunit test/test-math.js`. The output will show the results of all the test methods, specifying whether they passed successfully or not:

```
nodeunit test/test-math.js
    test-math.js
    test-math.js
  addTest
  subtractTest

OK: 2 assertions (5ms)
```

Let's modify `addTest` in such a way that it gets broken and to see how test failures are reported by the Nodeunit module:

```
exports.test_add = function (test) {
    test.equal(math.add(1, 1), 3);
    test.done();
};
```

Executing the test this time results in a failure with some assert failure messages, and in the end, there is an aggregation saying how many of the executed tests failed:

```
nodeunit test-math.js
test-math.js
  addTest
at Object.equal (/usr/lib/node_modules/nodeunit/lib/types.js:83:39)
at Object.exports.addTest (../hello-node/test/test-math.js:
(..)

AssertionError: 2 == 3
  subtractTest
FAILURES: 1/2 assertions failed (12ms)
```

We just created our Nodeunit's first unit test. However, it tests math function in a rather isolated way. I suppose you are wondering how we can use Nodeunit to test functions with complex arguments such as HTTP request and response, that are bound to a context. This is possible using so-called **mock objects**. They are a predefined version of the state of complex context-based arguments or functions, in objects that we want to use in our unit test in order to test the behavior of our module for the exact state of the object.

To use mock objects, we will need to install a module that supports object mocking. There are various types of testing tools and modules available out there. Most of them, however, are designed to test the JavaScript client functionality. There are modules such as JsMockito, a JavaScript fork of the famous Mockito framework for Java, and node-inspector, a module that provides a JavaScript debugger that starts implicitly in the Google Chrome browser.

Native support for the Chrome browser is logical, since Node.js is built on top of the Google V8 JavaScript Engine. As we are developing a server-side application, these are not the most convenient tools, as JsMockito is not pluggable as a Node.js module, and using a debugger within your browser to debug backed applications just doesn't seem right to me. Anyway, if you are about to dive deeper into Node.js, you should definitely give them a try.

For testing server-side JavaScript modules, we will use the Sinon.JS module. Like all the other modules, it is available in the npm repository, so execute the following command to install it:

```
npm install -g sinon
```

Sinon.JS is a very flexible JavaScript testing library providing functionality for mocking, stubbing, and spying on JavaScript objects. It is available at http://sinonjs.org and can be used with any JavaScript testing framework. Let's see what we need in order to test our HTTP module. It exports a single method, handleRequest, which takes the HTTP request and response objects as arguments. Based on the requested method, the module calls its internal functions to handle different requests. Each request handler writes a different output to the response.

To test this functionality in an isolated environment such as Nodeunit, we need mock objects, which will then be passed as arguments. To ensure that the module behaves as expected, we will need to have access to the data stored in those objects.

Working with mock objects

Here are the steps that need to be carried out when using mock objects:

1. Call the require function with sinon as a parameter and export a test function from it:

   ```
   var sinon = require('sinon');
   exports.testAPI(test){...}
   ```

2. Define an API description of the method you want to mock as follows:

   ```
   var api = {'methodX' : function () {},
     'methodY' : function() {},
     'methodZ' : function() {}};
   ```

3. Use sinon within the exported function in order to create mock objects out of the api description:

   ```
   var mock = sinon.mock(api);
   ```

4. Set the expectations on the mock objects. Expectations are set on the mocked objects by describing how the mocked method should behave, what arguments it is supposed to take, and what value it is supposed to return. When the mocked method is called with a different state than what is described, the expectation will fail when verified later:

```
mock.expects('methodX').once().withArgs('xyz')
.returns('abc');
api.methodX('xyz')
```

5. The preceding sample expects that methodX gets called exactly once with the xyz argument, and it will force the method to return abc. The Sinon.JS module makes that possible for us.

The method of the description object is called and not that of the mocked object. The mocked object is used to set the expectations for the mocked method, and later to check whether those expectations have been fulfilled.

6. Use the mocked object in the test environment and, later, call its verify() method. This method will check whether the code being tested interacted correctly with mock, that is, how many times the method has been called and whether it has been called with the expected arguments. If any of the expectations is not met, then an error will be thrown, causing the test to fail.

7. The exported test function of our test module has an argument. That argument provides assert methods that can be used to check test conditions. In our example, we mocked the method to always return abc when called with the 'xyz' arguments. So, to complete the test, the following assert can be done, and in the end, the mock object needs to be verified:

```
mock.expects('methodX').once().withArgs('xyz')
.returns('abc');
test.equals(api.methodX('xyz'), 'abc');
mock.verify();
```

8. Try modifying the arguments passed to methodX such that they don't match the expectation, and you will see this breaking your test.

9. Let's put these steps into practice and create the following `test-http-module.js` file in the `test` directory:

```javascript
var sinon = require('sinon');
exports.handleGetRequestTest =  (test) => {
  var response = {'writeHead' :  () => {}, 'end': () => {}};
  var responseMock = sinon.mock(response);
    responseMock.expects('end').once().withArgs('Get action was
requested');
    responseMock.expects('writeHead').once().withArgs(200, {
      'Content-Type' : 'text/plain'});

  var request = {};
  var requestMock = sinon.mock(request);
  requestMock.method = 'GET';

  var http_module = require('../modules/http-module');
  http_module.handleRequest(requestMock, response);
  responseMock.verify();
  test.done();
};
```

10. Start the test with Nodeunit's `test-http-module.js` to verify that it passes successfully. Your next step will be to extend the test so that it covers the handling of all the HTTP methods in our HTTP module:

```
nodeunit test/test-http-module.js

test-http-module.js
Request processing completed
 handleGetRequestTest

OK: 0 assertions (32ms)
```

Deploying an application

Node.js has an event-driven, non-blocking I/O model, which makes it perfect for real-time applications that scale well in distributed environments, such as public or private cloud platforms. Each cloud platform offers tools that allow seamless deployment, distribution, and scaling of its hosted applications. In this section, we will look at two publicly available Node.js application cloud providers—Nodejitsu and Microsoft Azure.

But first, let's spend some time on the clustering support, as it is fundamental for understanding why Node.js fits so well into the cloud environment. Node.js comes with clustering support built in to its core. Using the cluster module in your applications allows them to start as many workers as necessary to handle the load they will face. Generally, it is recommended to match the number of workers to the number of threads or logical cores your environment has.

 The heart of your application is the master process. It is responsible for keeping a registry of active workers and the load of the application, and how to create it. It also creates more workers when needed and reduces them when the load decreases.

The cloud platform should also ensure that there is zero downtime when deploying new versions of the applications. In such cases, the master process needs to be notified that a newer version should be distributed. It should fork the new workers' new application version, and notify the workers currently running with the old version to close their listeners; thus, it stops accepting connections and exits gracefully once they finish. Thus, all the new incoming requests will be handled by the newly-started workers, and after the obsolete workers terminate, all the running workers will be running the latest version.

Nodejitsu

Let's take a closer look at some of the Node.js **Platform as a Service (PaaS)** offerings. The first PaaS we will look at is Nodejitsu, available at `https://www.nodejitsu.com`.

This allows seamless deployment of Node.js applications on the cloud, with many useful features for development, management, deployment, and monitoring of Node.js applications. To interact with jitsu, you need to install its command-line interface, which is available as a Node.js module:

```
npm install -g jitsu
```

After installing jitsu and starting it with `jitsu`, you will be given a warm welcome, with a friendly console screen that will introduce you to the basic jitsu commands, as follows:

```
●●● valio@G771JW: ~
valio@G771JW:~$ jitsu
warn:
warn:     Nodejitsu has been acquired by GoDaddy
warn:
warn:     Read more at: https://nodejitsu.com/godaddy
warn:     Or run:         jitsu godaddy
warn:
info:     Welcome to Nodejitsu
info:     jitsu v0.15.0, node v8.10.0
info:     It worked if it ends with Nodejitsu ok
info:     Executing command
help:
help:      _ _ _____ _____ _ _
help:     | | |_   _/  ___| | | |
help:     _| | | | | \ `--.| | | |
help:
help:     Flawless deployment of Node.js apps to the cloud
help:     open-source and fully customizable.
help:     https://github.com/nodejitsu/jitsu
help:
help:     Usage:
help:
help:        jitsu <resource> <action> <param1> <param2> ...
help:
help:     Common Commands:
```

In order to interact with jitsu, you will need to sign up for it. Jitsu offers different pricing plans, as well as free trial services.

You can do that either from their website or with the `jitsu signup` command. Then you can start making use of the tools the command-line interface offers.

Microsoft Azure

Microsoft's cloud platform as a service, Azure, also offers hosting of Node.js applications. They have chosen a slightly different approach, and instead of providing a command-line interface to interact with their repositories, they make use of their Git integration; that is, you interact with Azure as you would interact with any other Git repository. If you are not familiar with Git, I strongly recommend that you learn more about this distributed source code version control system.

If you've chosen Azure as your platform, you will find the following link very useful: `http://azure.microsoft.com/en-us/develop/nodejs/`.

Heroku

Heroku is a public cloud offering that allows you to manage, deploy, and scale Node.js applications. Preparing your Node application for the Heroku environment does not take too much effort, as long as you install its command-line interface, available either at `https://devcenter.heroku.com/articles/heroku-cli` or through your package manager with the following:

```
npm install -g heroku-cli
```

All you have to do is provide a `'start script'` element in the `package.json` file, push it to your relevant origin Git repository using `git push master heroku`, then log in and create your application, using the `heroku login` and `heroku create` commands.

Self-test questions

To get additional confidence about your newly-gained knowledge, go through the next set of statements and state whether they are true or false:

1. Node modules can export more than one function to outer components
2. Node modules are extensible
3. Modules always need to explicitly declare their dependencies to other modules
4. When using mocking in a test environment, the mocked method is called on the mocked object
5. Debugging Node.js code is not as straightforward as other pieces of non-JavaScript code

Summary

In this chapter, you gained your first Node.js experience, starting from a simple `Hello world` application and moving on to a more complex sample HTTP server-like application that handles incoming HTTP requests. Being more confident with Node.js, you refactored the application to use user modules, and then created unit tests for your module using a mocking framework to eliminate dependencies on complex objects in your test environment.

Now that you've understood how to handle and test incoming HTTP requests, in the next chapter, our next step will be to define what a typical web API looks like and how it can be tested.

Building a Typical Web API 3

Our first draft API will be a read-only version and will not support creating or updating items in the catalog as real-world applications do. Instead, we will concentrate on the API definition itself, and will worry about data storage later on. Of course, using file storage for data exposed to millions of users is anything but an option, so a database layer will be provided to our application further in the book, after we have looked into modern NoSQL database solutions.

We will also cover the topic of content negotiation, a mechanism that allows consumers to specify the expected format of requested data. Finally, we will take a look at several ways to expose different versions of a service, in case it evolves in a backward-incompatible way.

To sum up, in this chapter, you will learn the following:

- How to specify a web API
- How to implement routes
- How to query your API
- Content negotiation
- API versioning

After this chapter, you should be able to completely specify a RESTful API and will be almost ready to start implementing real-life Node.js RESTful services.

Specifying the API

The very first thing a project usually starts with is a definition of the operations the API will expose. According to the REST principles, an operation is exposed by an HTTP method and a URI. The action performed by each operation should not contradict the natural meaning of its HTTP method. The following table specifies the operations of our API in detail:

Method	URI	Description
GET	/category	Retrieves all available categories in the catalog.
GET	/category/{category-id}/	Retrieves all the items available under a specific category.
GET	/category/{category-id}/{item-id}	Retrieves an item by its ID under a specific category.
POST	/category	Creates a new category; if it exists, it will update it.
POST	/category/{category-id}/	Creates a new item in a specified category. If the item exists, it will update it.
PUT	/category/{category-id}	Updates a category.
PUT	/category/{category-id}/{item-id}	Updates an item in a specified category.
DELETE	/category/{category-id}	Deletes an existing category.
DELETE	/category/{category-id}/{item-id}	Deletes an item in a specified category.

The second step is to choose an appropriate format for our catalog application's data. JSON objects are natively supported by JavaScript. They are easy to extend during the evolution of an application and are consumable by almost any platform available. Thus, the JSON format seems to be our logical choice for us. Here is the JSON representation of an item, and category objects that will be used throughout this book:

```
{
    "itemId": "item-identifier-1",
    "itemName": "Sports Watch",
    "category": "Watches",
    "categoryId": 1,
```

```
        "price": 150,
        "currency": "EUR"
    }

    {
        "categoryName" : "Watches",
        "categoryId" : "1",
        "itemsCount" : 100,
        "items" : [{
                "itemId" : "item-identifier-1",
                "itemName":"Sports Watch",
                "price": 150,
                "currency" : "EUR"
            }]
    }
```

So far, our API has defined a set of operations and the data format to be used. The next step is to implement a module that will export functions serving each of the operations in the route.

To begin with, let's create a new Node.js Express project. Select a directory where your projects will be stored and from your shell Terminal, execute express chapter3. If you are using Windows, you will need to install the express-generator module before generating the project. The express-generator will create your an initial express project layout in the selected directory. This layout provides the default project structure for you, ensuring that your Express project follows the standard project structure. It makes your project easier to navigate.

The next step is to import the project into the Atom IDE. Right-click anywhere in the **Projects** tab and select **Add project folder** then select the directory Express generated for you.

As you can see, Express has done some background work for us and has created a starting point for our application: app.js. It has also created the package.json file for us. Let's take a look at each of these files, starting with package.json:

```
{
  "name": "chapter3",
  "version": "1.0.0",
  "description": "",
  "main": "app.js",
  "scripts": {
    "test": "test"
  },
  "author": "",
```

```
   "license": "ISC",
  "dependencies": {
 "dependencies": {
     "body-parser": "~1.13.2",
     "cookie-parser": "~1.3.5",
     "debug": "~2.2.0",
     "express": "~4.16.1",
     "jade": "~1.11.0",
     "morgan": "~1.6.1",
     "serve-favicon": "~2.3.0"

  }
 }
```

As we created a blank Node.js Express project, we initially have dependencies only to the Express framework, some middleware modules such as `morgan`, `body-parser`, and `cookie-parser`, and the Jade template language. Jade is a straightforward template language used to produce HTML code inside templates. If you are interested in it, you can find out more about it at `http://www.jade-lang.com`.

The current version of the Express framework at the time of writing is 4.16.1; to update it, execute `npm install express@4.16.1 --save` from the `chapter3` directory. This command will update the dependency of the application to the desired version. The `--save` option will update and save the new version of the dependency in the project's `package.json` file.

 When you introduce new module dependencies, it is up to you to keep the `package.json` file up to date in order to maintain an accurate state of the modules your application depends on.

We will come to what middleware modules are a bit later in the chapter.

For now, we will ignore the content of the `public` and `view` directories as it is not relevant to our RESTful service. They contain the auto-generated stylesheets and template files that might be helpful, if we decide to develop a web-based consumer of the services at a later stage.

We've already mentioned that the Express project created a starting point for our web application in `app.js`. Let's take a deeper look at it:

```javascript
var express = require('express');
var path = require('path');
var favicon = require('serve-favicon');
var logger = require('morgan');
var cookieParser = require('cookie-parser');
var bodyParser = require('body-parser');

var routes = require('./routes/index');
var users = require('./routes/users');

var app = express();

// view engine setup
app.set('views', path.join(__dirname, 'views'));
app.set('view engine', 'jade');

// uncomment after placing your favicon in /public
//app.use(favicon(path.join(__dirname, 'public', 'favicon.ico')));
app.use(logger('dev'));
app.use(bodyParser.json());
app.use(bodyParser.urlencoded({ extended: false }));
app.use(cookieParser());
app.use(express.static(path.join(__dirname, 'public')));

app.use('/', routes);
app.use('/users', users);

// catch 404 and forward to error handler
app.use(function(req, res, next) {
  var err = new Error('Not Found');
  err.status = 404;
  next(err);
});

// error handlers

// development error handler
// will print stacktrace
if (app.get('env') === 'development') {
  app.use(function(err, req, res, next) {
    res.status(err.status || 500);
    res.render('error', {
      message: err.message,
      error: err
```

```
      });
    });
  }

  // production error handler
  // no stacktraces leaked to user
  app.use(function(err, req, res, next) {
    res.status(err.status || 500);
    res.render('error', {
      message: err.message,
      error: {}
    });
  });
```

```
  module.exports = app;
```

Obviously, the Express generator has done a lot for us as it has instantiated the Express framework and has assigned a complete development environment around it. It has done the following:

- Configured the middleware to be used in our application, `body-parser`, the default router, as well as error handler middleware for our development environment
- Injected a logger instance of the morgan middleware module
- Configured the Jade template, as it has been selected as the default template for our application
- Configured the default URI that our Express application will be listening to, `/` and `/users`, and created dummy handle functions for them

You will have to install all the modules used in `app.js` in order to start the generated application successfully. Also, make sure you update the dependencies of your `package.json` file using the `--save` option after installing them.

The Express generator also created a starting script for the application. It is under the `bin/www` directory of your project and looks like the following snippet:

```
  #!/usr/bin/env node

  /**
   * Module dependencies.
   */

  var app = require('../app');
  var debug = require('debug')('chapter3:server');
```

```
var http = require('http');

/**
 * Get port from environment and store in Express.
 */

var port = normalizePort(process.env.PORT || '3000');
app.set('port', port);

/**
 * Create HTTP server.
 */

var server = http.createServer(app);

/**
 * Listen on provided port, on all network interfaces.
 */

server.listen(port);
server.on('error', onError);
server.on('listening', onListening);

/**
 * Normalize a port into a number, string, or false.
 */

function normalizePort(val) {
  var port = parseInt(val, 10);

  if (isNaN(port)) {
    // named pipe
    return val;
  }

  if (port >= 0) {
    // port number
    return port;
  }

  return false;
}

/**
 * Event listener for HTTP server "error" event.
 */

function onError(error) {
```

```
  if (error.syscall !== 'listen') {
    throw error;
  }

  var bind = typeof port === 'string'
    ? 'Pipe ' + port
    : 'Port ' + port;

  // handle specific listen errors with friendly messages
  switch (error.code) {
    case 'EACCES':
      console.error(bind + ' requires elevated privileges');
      process.exit(1);
      break;
    case 'EADDRINUSE':
      console.error(bind + ' is already in use');
      process.exit(1);
      break;
    default:
      throw error;
  }
}

/**
 * Event listener for HTTP server "listening" event.
 */

function onListening() {
  var addr = server.address();
  var bind = typeof addr === 'string'
    ? 'pipe ' + addr
    : 'port ' + addr.port;
  debug('Listening on ' + bind);
}
```

To start the application, execute `node bin/www`; this will execute the script above and will start the Node.js application. So requesting `http://localhost:3000` in your browser will result in calling the default `GET` handler, which gives a warm welcome response:

Default welcome message from an Express application

The generator created a dummy `routes/users.js`; it exposes a route linked to a dummy module available at the `/users` location. Requesting it will result in calling the `list` function of the user's route, which outputs a static response: `respond with a resource`.

Our application will not be using a template language and style sheets, so let's get rid of the lines that set the views and view engine properties in the application configuration. In addition, we will be implementing our own routes. Thus, we don't need the binding of the `/` and `/users` URIs for our app, neither do we need the `user` module; instead, we will utilize a `catalog` module and from a route:

```
var express = require('express');
var path = require('path');
var favicon = require('serve-favicon');
var logger = require('morgan');
var cookieParser = require('cookie-parser');
var bodyParser = require('body-parser');

var routes = require('./routes/index');
var catalog = require('./routes/catalog')
var app = express();

//uncomment after placing your favicon in /public
//app.use(favicon(path.join(__dirname, 'public', 'favicon.ico')));
```

```
app.use(logger('dev'));
app.use(bodyParser.json());
app.use(bodyParser.urlencoded({ extended: false }));
app.use(cookieParser());
app.use(express.static(path.join(__dirname, 'public')));

app.use('/', routes);
app.use('/catalog', catalog);


// catch 404 and forward to error handler
app.use(function(req, res, next) {
  var err = new Error('Not Found');
  err.status = 404;
  next(err);
});

//development error handler will print stacktrace
if (app.get('env') === 'development') {
  app.use(function(err, req, res, next) {
    res.status(err.status || 500);
    res.render('error', {
      message: err.message,
      error: err
    });
  });
}

// production error handler no stacktraces leaked to user
app.use(function(err, req, res, next) {
  res.status(err.status || 500);
  res.render('error', {
    message: err.message,
    error: {}
  });
});

module.exports = app;
```

So after this cleanup, our application looks a lot cleaner and we are ready to move forward.

Before doing that, though, there is one term that needs further explanation: middleware. It is a subset of chained functions called by the `Express.js` routing layer before a user-defined handler is invoked. Middleware functions have full access to the `request` and `response` objects and can modify either of them. The middleware chain is always called in the exact order in which it has been defined, so it is vital for you to know exactly what a specific piece of middleware is doing. Once a middleware function finishes, it calls the next function in the chain by invoking its next argument as a function. After the complete chain gets executed, the user-defined request handler is called.

Here are the basic rules that apply to the middleware chain:

- A middleware function has the following signature: `function (request, response, next)`.
- Middleware functions are executed in the exact order in which they have been added to the application chain. This means that if you want your middleware function to be called before a specific route, you need to add it before declaring the route.
- Middleware functions use their third parameter, `next`, as a function to indicate that they have completed their work and to exit. When the `next()` parameter of the last function in the chain has been called, the chained execution is completed and the `request` and the `response` objects reach the defined handlers, in the state set by the middleware.

Now that we know what a middleware function is, let's clarify what the currently used middleware functions provide our application with. The `body-parser` middleware is the Express framework built in a parser. It parses the `request` body and populates the `request` object after the middleware execution finishes, that is, it provides JSON payload handling.

Now it is time to move on and implement our user module that will be mapped to our URIs. The module will be named `modules/catalog.js`:

```
var fs = require('fs');

function readCatalogSync() {
   var file = './data/catalog.json';
   if (fs.existsSync(file)) {
     var content = fs.readFileSync(file);
     var catalog = JSON.parse(content);
     return catalog;
```

```
    }
    return undefined;
  }

exports.findItems = function(categoryId) {
  console.log('Returning all items for categoryId: ' + categoryId);
  var catalog = readCatalogSync();
  if (catalog) {
    var items = [];
    for (var index in catalog.catalog) {
        if (catalog.catalog[index].categoryId === categoryId) {
          var category = catalog.catalog[index];
          for (var itemIndex in category.items) {
            items.push(category.items[itemIndex]);
          }
        }
    }
    return items;
  }
  return undefined;
}

exports.findItem = function(categoryId, itemId) {
  console.log('Looking for item with id' + itemId);
  var catalog = readCatalogSync();
  if (catalog) {
    for (var index in catalog.catalog) {
        if (catalog.catalog[index].categoryId === categoryId) {
          var category = catalog.catalog[index];
          for (var itemIndex in category.items) {
            if (category.items[itemIndex].itemId === itemId) {
              return category.items[itemIndex];
            }
          }
        }
    }
  }
  return undefined;
}

exports.findCategoryies = function() {
  console.log('Returning all categories');
  var catalog = readCatalogSync();
  if (catalog) {
    var categories = [];
    for (var index in catalog.catalog) {
        var category = {};
        category["categoryId"] = catalog.catalog[index].categoryId;
```

```
        category["categoryName"] = catalog.catalog[index].categoryName;

        categories.push(category);
    }
    return categories;
  }
  return [];
}
```

The catalog module is built around the `catalog.json` file, stored in the `data` directory. The content of the source file is read synchronously using the File System module, `fs`, within the `readCatalogSync` function. The File System module provides multiple useful filesystem operations such as functions for creating, renaming, or deleting files or directories; truncating; linking; `chmod` functions; as well as synchronous and asynchronous file access for reading and writing data. In our sample application, we aim to use the most straightforward approach, so we implement functions that read the `catalog.json` file by utilizing the `readFileSync` function of the File System module. It returns the content of a file as a string, within a synchronous call. All other functions of the module are exported and can be used to query the content of the source file, based on different criteria.

The catalog module exports the following functions:

- `findCategories`: This returns an array of JSON objects containing all the categories in the `catalog.json` file
- `findItems (categoryId)`: This returns an array JSON objects representing all the items in a given category
- `findItem(categoryId, itemId)`: This returns a JSON object representing a single item in a given category

Now that we have three complete functions, let's see how to bind them to our Express application.

Implementing routes

In Node.js terms, a route is a binding between a URI and function. The Express framework provides built-in support for routing. An `express` object instance contains functions named after each HTTP verb: `get`, `post`, `put`, and `delete`. They have the following syntax: `function(uri, handler);`. They are used to bind a handler function to a specific HTTP action executed over a URI. The handler function usually takes two arguments: `request` and `response`. Let's see it with a simple `Hello route` application:

```
var express = require('express');
var app = express();

app.get('/hello', function(request, response){
  response.send('Hello route');
});

app.listen(3000);
```

Running this sample at localhost and accessing `http://localhost:3000/hello` will result in calling your handler function and it will respond saying `Hello route`, but routing can give you much more. It allows you to define a URI with parameters; for example, let's use `/hello/:name` as a routing string. It tells the framework that the URI used consists of two parts: a static part (`hello`) and a variable part (the `name` parameter).

Furthermore, when the routing string and the handler function are defined in line with the `get` function of an Express instance, a parameter collection is made available directly in the `request` argument of the handler function. To demonstrate this, let's modify our previous example a bit:

```
var express = require('express');
var app = express();

app.get('/hello:name', function(request, response){
  response.send('Hello ' + request.params.name);
});

app.listen(3000);
```

As you can see in the preceding code snippet, we used a colon (`:`) to separate the parameter part of the URI from the static part. You can have multiple parameters in an Express route; for example, `/category/:category-id/items/:item-id` defines a route for displaying an item that belongs to a category, where the `category-id` and `item-id` are parameters.

Now let's try it out. Requesting `http://localhost:3000/hello/friend` will result in the following output:

```
hello friend
```

This is how we can provide parameterized URIs with Express. It is a nice feature, but it is often not enough. In web applications, we are used to providing additional parameters with GET parameters.

Unfortunately, the Express framework is not so good with GET parameters. Thus, we have to utilize the `url` module. It is built into Node.js to provide an easy way of using URL parsing. Let's use our `hello` result with other parameters in the application again, but extend it in a way that it outputs `hello all` when `/hello` is requested and `hello friend` when the requested URI is `/hello?name=friend`:

```
var express = require('express');
var url = require('url');
var app = express();

app.get('/hello', function(request, response){
    var getParams = url.parse(request.url, true).query;

    if (Object.keys(getParams).length == 0) {
        response.end('Hello all');
    } else {

        response.end('Hello ' + getParams.name);
    }
});

app.listen(3000);
```

There are a few things worth mentioning here. We used the `url` module's function `parse`. It takes a URL as its first argument and a Boolean as an optional second argument, which specifies whether the query string should be parsed or not. The `url.parse` function returns an associative object. We used `Object.keys` with it to transform the keys in these associative objects into an array so that we can check its length. This will help us check whether our URI has been called with GET parameters or not. In addition to the routing functions named after each HTTP verb, there is also a function named `all`. When used, it routes all the HTTP actions to the specified URI.

Now that we know how routing and the GET parameters work within Node.js and the Express environment, we are ready to define a route for the catalog module and bind it in our application. The following is the route as defined in routes/catalog.js.

```
var express = require('express');
var catalog = require('../modules/catalog.js')

var router = express.Router();

router.get('/', function(request, response, next) {
  var categories = catalog.findCategoryies();
  response.json(categories);
});

router.get('/:categoryId', function(request, response, next) {
  var categories = catalog.findItems(request.params.categoryId);
  if (categories === undefined) {
    response.writeHead(404, {'Content-Type' : 'text/plain'});
    response.end('Not found');
  } else {
    response.json(categories);
  }
});

router.get('/:categoryId/:itemId', function(request, response, next) {
  var item = catalog.findItem(request.params.categoryId,
request.params.itemId);
  if (item === undefined) {
    response.writeHead(404, {'Content-Type' : 'text/plain'});
    response.end('Not found');
  } else {
  response.json(item);
  }
});
module.exports = router;
```

First, a Router instance is created from the Express module. Here is a table that nicely describes the routing we just implemented. This will be helpful later when we test our API:

HTTP method	Route	Catalog's module function
GET	/catalog	findCategories()
GET	/catalog/:categoryId	findItems(categoryId)
GET	/catalog/:categoryId/:itemId	findItem(categoryId, itemId)

Querying the API using test data

We need some test data in order to test our service, so let's use the `catalog.json` file in the `data` directory of our project. This data will allow us to test all our three functions, but to do that, we would need a client that can send REST requests against an endpoint. If you still haven't created a Postman project for testing your application, now is an appropriate time to create it.

Requesting `/catalog` should return all the categories in the `test` file:

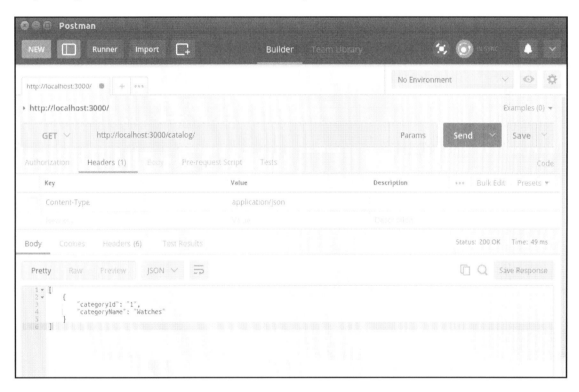

Thus, requesting `/catalog/1` should result in returning a list with all the items under the `Watches` category:

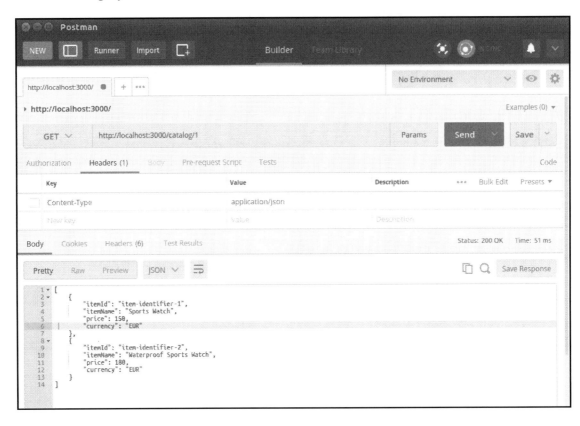

Finally, requesting `http://localhost:3000/catalog/1/item-identifier-1` would display only the item identified by `item-identifier-1`, and requesting a nonexistent item would result in response with status code `404`:

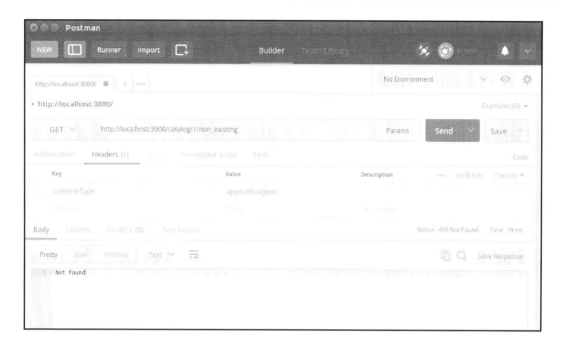

Content negotiation

So far, the catalog service supports only the JSON format, and thus works only with the media type `application/json`. Let's assume our service has to offer data in different formats, for example, both JSON and XML. Then, the consumer needs to explicitly define the data format they need. The best way to carry out content negotiation in REST has been a very debatable subject for a long time.

In his famous discussion on implementing content negotiation correctly, Roy Fielding states the following:

> *All important resources must have URIs.*

However, that leaves a gap on how to expose the same resource in a different data format, so Roy continues with the following:

> *Agent-driven negotiation is far more effective, but there was a huge disagreement between myself and the chair of the HTTP working group and my original agent-driven design for HTTP/1.1 was effectively buried in committee. To do negotiation right, the client needs to be aware of all the alternatives and what it should use as a bookmark.*

While one can still choose to stick with a URI-driven negotiation by providing the desired format with custom GET parameters, the REST community has chosen to stick to Roy's suggestion for agent-driven negotiation. Now that it has been almost a decade since this argument was initiated, it has been proven that they took the right decision. Agent-driven negotiation makes use of the Accept HTTP header.

The Accept HTTP header specifies the media type of the resource that the consumer is willing to process. In addition to the Accept header, the consumer may also make use of the Accept-Language and Accept-Encoding headers to specify what language and encoding the results should be provided in. If the server fails to provide the results in the expected format, it can either return a default value or make use of HTTP 406 Not acceptable in order not to cause data confusion errors on the client side.

The Node.js HTTP response object contains a method, format, that performs content negotiation based on the Accept HTTP header if set in the request object. It uses the built-in request.accepts() to select an appropriate handler for the request. If that is not found, the server invokes the default handler, which responds with HTTP 406 Not acceptable. Let's create a demo on how to use the format method within one of our routes. For that purpose, let's assume we have implemented a function within our catalog module, named list_groups_in_xml, that provides the group data in XML format:

```
app.get('/catalog', function(request, response) {
    response.format( {
        'text/xml' : function() {
            response.send(catalog.findCategoiesXml());
        },
        'application/json' : function() {
            response.json(catalog.findCategoriesJson());
        },
        'default' : function() {.
            response.status(406).send('Not Acceptable');
        }
    });
});
```

This is how you can implement content negotiation in a clear and straightforward way.

API versioning

It is an inevitable fact that all application APIs evolve. However, the evolution of public APIs with an unknown number of consumers, such as RESTful services, is a sensitive topic. As consumers may not be able to handle the modified data appropriately and there is no way of notifying all of them, we need to keep our APIs as backward-compatible as possible. One way to do so is to use different URIs for different versions of our application. Currently, our catalog API is available at `/catalog`.

When the time is right for a new version, for example, Version 2, we may need to keep the previous version available at another URI for backward-compatibility. Best practice is to encode the version number in the URI, such as `/v1/catalog`, and keep `/catalog` mapped to the latest version. Thus, requesting `/catalog` will cause a redirect to `/v2/catalog` and will make use of the HTTP `3xx` status codes to indicate the redirection to the latest version.

Another option for versioning would be to keep the URI of your API stable and rely on custom HTTP headers that will specify the version. But that's not very stable approach concerning backward-compatibility as it is much more natural to modify a URL of a request in an application rather than modify the headers that are sent within the request.

Self-test questions

To get additional confidence, go through this set of statements and state whether they are true or false:

1. A REST-enabled endpoint must support all HTTP methods relevant to the REST principles
2. When content negotiation fails, due to an unsupported media type passed as a value of the accepts header, 301 is the appropriate status code.
3. When using parameterized routes, the developer can specify the type of the parameter, for example, whether it is a numeric or a literal type.

Summary

In this chapter, we dived into some more complex topics. Let's sum up what we covered. We started by specifying the operations of our web API and defined that an operation is a combination of a URI and HTTP action. Next, we implemented routes and bound them to an operation. Then, we requested each operation using the Postman REST client to request the URIs that we routed. In the content negotiation section, we handled the `Accept` HTTP header to provide the results in the format requested by consumers. Finally, we covered the topic of API versions, which allow us to develop backward-compatible APIs.

We used old-fashioned filesystem storage for our data in this chapter. This is not suitable for a web application. Thus, we will look into modern, scalable, and reliable NoSQL storage in the next chapter.

4
Using NoSQL Databases

In the last chapter, we implemented a sample application exposing a read-only service that provided catalog data. For the sake of simplicity, we introduced a performance bottleneck in this implementation by using file storage. This storage is not suitable for web applications. It relies on 33 physical files, preventing our application from servicing heavy loads, as file storage lacks multitenant support due to disc I/O operations. In other words, we definitely need to look for a better storage solution, which scales easily, when needed, following the demands of our REST-enabled application. NoSQL databases are now heavily used in web and in cloud environments, ensuring zero downtime and high availability. They have the following advantages over traditional transactional SQL databases:

- They **support schema versions**; that is, they can work with object representations rather than filling the object state based on definitions of one or several tables.
- They are **extensible**, because they store an actual object. Data evolution is supported implicitly, so all you need to do is call the operation that stores the modified object.
- They are designed to be **highly distributed** and **scalable**.

Nearly all modern NoSQL solutions out there support clustering and can scale further, along with the load of your application. Additionally, most of them have REST-enabled interfaces over HTTP, which eases their usage over a load balancer in high-availability scenarios. Classical database drivers are usually not available for traditional client-side languages, such as JavaScript, because they require native libraries or drivers. However, the idea of NoSQL originated from using document data stores. Thus, most of them support the JSON format, which is native to JavaScript. Last but not least, most NoSQL solutions are open source and are available for free, with all the benefits that open source projects offer: community, examples, and freedom!

In this chapter, we will take a look at the MongoDB NoSQL database and the Mongoose module that interacts with it. We will see how to design and implement automated tests for the database models. Finally, at the end of the chapter, we will remove the file storage bottleneck and will move our application to an almost ready for production state.

MongoDB – a document store database

MongoDB is an open source document database with built-in support for the JSON format. It provides a full index support, based on any of the available attributes in a document. It is ideal for high-availability scenarios due to its scalability features. MongoDB, available at `https://mms.mongodb.com`, is cloud-ready with its management services, **MongoDB Management Services (MMS)**. They utilize and automate most development operations that need to be carried out to keep your cloud database in good shape, taking care of upgrades, further scaling, backups, recovery, performance, and security alerts.

Let's move forward and install MongoDB. Installers for Windows, Linux, macOS, and Solaris are available at `http://www.mongodb.org/downloads`. Linux users can find MongoDB in all popular distribution repositories, while Windows users can make use of a user-friendly wizard which will guide you through the installation steps, where, for a typical installation, all you need to do is accept the license agreement and provide an installation path.

After a successful installation, execute the following command to start MongoDB. If you want to specify a custom location for your data, you have to use the `--dbpath` argument. Optionally, you can start the MongoDB HTTP console via the `--rest` argument:

```
mongod --dbpath ./data --rest
```

The default port for communicating with MongoDB is `27017`, and its HTTP console is implicitly configured to use a port higher than the data port by a value of 1,000. Therefore, the default port of the console will be `28017`. The HTTP console provides useful information about the database, such as logs, health status, available databases, and so on. I strongly advise you to spend some time with it. The console can also be used as a RESTful health check service of the database, because it provides JSON-encoded information about the running database services and the last error that occurred:

```
GET /replSetGetStatus?text=1 HTTP/1.1
Host: localhost:28017
Connection: Keep-Alive
User-Agent: RestClient-Tool
HTTP/1.0 200 OK
Content-Length: 56
Connection: close
Content-Type: text/plain;charset=utf-8
{
"ok": 0,
"errmsg": "not running with --replSet"
}
```

This REST interface can be used in a script or an application to automate altering notifications providing the current state of the database engine and so on.

The log section of the console shows that your server is running successfully (if it is). Now we are ready to move further and see how to connect Node.js to MongoDB.

Database modeling with Mongoose

Mongoose is a module that connects Node.js to MongoDB in an **object document mapper (ODM)** style. It offers the **Create, Read, Update, and Delete** (also known as **CRUD**) functionalities for documents stored in the database. Mongoose defines the structure of the used documents using schemas. The schema is the smallest unit of data definition in Mongoose. A model is built out of a schema definition. It is a constructor-like function that can be used to create or query documents. Documents are instances of a model and represent one-to-one mapping to the documents stored in MongoDB. The schema-model-document hierarchy provides a self-descriptive way of defining objects and allows easy data validation.

Let's start by installing Mongoose with npm:

```
npm install mongoose
```

Now that we have the Mongoose module installed, our first step will be to define a schema that will represent an item in the catalog:

```
var mongoose = require('mongoose');
var Schema = mongoose.Schema;
var itemSchema = new Schema ({
    "itemId" : {type: String, index: {unique: true}},
    "itemName": String,
    "price": Number,
    "currency" : String,
    "categories": [String]
});
```

The preceding code snippet creates a schema definition of an item. Defining a schema is straightforward and is quite similar to JSON schema definition; you have to describe and attribute with its type and optionally provide additional properties for each key. In the case of the catalog application, we need to use the itemId as a unique index in order to avoid having two different items with the same ID. Thus, apart from defining its type as String, we also use the index attribute to describe that the value of the itemId field must be unique for each individual item.

Mongoose introduces the term **model**. A model is a constructor-like function compiled out of a schema definition. An instance of a model represents a document that can be saved to or read from the database. Creating a model instance is done by calling the `model` function of a `mongoose` instance and passing the schema that the model should use:

```
var CatalogItem = mongoose.model('Item', itemSchema);
```

A model also exposes functions for querying and data manipulations. Assuming that we have initialized a schema and created a model, storing a new item to MongoDB is as simple as creating a new `model` instance and invoking its `save` function:

```
var mongoose = require('mongoose');

mongoose.connect('mongodb://localhost/catalog');
var db = mongoose.connection;

db.on('error', console.error.bind(console, 'connection error:'));
db.once('open', function() {
  var watch = new CatalogItem({
    itemId: 9 ,
    itemName: "Sports Watch1",
    brand: 'A1',
    price: 100,
    currency: "EUR",
    categories: ["Watches", "Sports Watches"]
  });

  watch.save((error, item, affectedNo)=> {
    if (!error) {
      console.log('Item added successfully to the catalog');
    } else {
      console.log('Cannot add item to the catlog');
    }
  });
});

db.once('open', function() {
  var filter = {
    'itemName' : 'Sports Watch1',
    'price': 100
  }

  CatalogItem.find(filter, (error, result) => {
    if (error) {
      consoloe.log('Error occured');
    } else {
      console.log('Results found:'+ result.length);
```

```
      console.log(result);
    }
  });
});
```

Here is how to use the model in order to query for documents representing a sports watch belonging to the Watches group named Sports Watches:

```
db.once('open', function() {
  var filter = {
    'itemName' : 'Sports Watch1',
    'price': 100
  }
  CatalogItem.findOne(filter, (error, result) => {
    if (error) {
      consoloe.log('Error occurred');
    } else {
      console.log(result);
    }
  });
});
```

The model also exposes a findOne function, a convenient way of finding an object by its unique index and then performing some data manipulation on it, that is, for delete or update operations. The following example deletes an item:

```
CatalogItem.findOne({itemId: 1 }, (error, data) => {
  if (error) {
    console.log(error);
    return;
  } else {
    if (!data) {
    console.log('not found');
      return;
    } else {
      data.remove(function(error){
        if (!error) { data.remove(); }
        else { console.log(error); }
        });
    }
  }
});
```

Testing a Mongoose model with Mocha

Mocha is one of the most popular testing frameworks for JavaScript; its main goal is to provide an easy way to test asynchronous JavaScript code. Let's install Mocha globally so that we can make it available to any Node.js application that we may develop in the future:

```
npm install -g mocha
```

We will also need an assertion library that can be used together with Mocha. The assertion library provides functions for validating actual values, against expected ones, when they are not equal, the assertion library will cause test failure. Should.js assertion library module is easy to use and it will be our choice, so let's install it globally too:

```
npm install -g should
```

Now that we have our testing modules installed, we need to specify our testcase file path in the package.json file. Let's modify it by adding a test element pointing to Mocha and the testcase file in the script node:

```json
{
"name": "chapter4",
"version": "0.0.0",
"private": true,
"scripts": {
"start": "node ./bin/www",
"test": "mocha test/model-test.js"
 },
"dependencies": {
"body-parser": "~1.13.2",
"cookie-parser": "~1.3.5",
"debug": "~2.2.0",
"express": "~4.16.0",
"jade": "~1.11.0",
"morgan": "~1.6.1",
"serve-favicon": "~2.3.0"
 }
}
```

This will tell the npm package manager to trigger Mocha when the npm test is executed.

Automation of Mongoose tests must not be affected by the current state of the database. To ensure that the results are predictable at each test run, we need to ensure that the database state is exactly as we would expect it. We will implement a module called prepare.js in the test directory. It will clear the database before each test run:

```
var mongoose = require('mongoose');
beforeEach(function (done) {
  function clearDatabase() {
    for (var i in mongoose.connection.collections) {
      mongoose.connection.collections[i].remove(function()
      {});
    }
    return done();
  }
  if (mongoose.connection.readyState === 0) {
    mongoose.connect(config.db.test, function (err) {
      if (err) {
        throw err;
      }
      return clearDatabase();
    });
  } else {
    return clearDatabase();
  }
});
afterEach(function (done) {
  mongoose.disconnect();
  return done();
});
```

Next, we will implement a Mocha test, which creates a new item:

```
var mongoose = require('mongoose');
var should = require('should');
var prepare = require('./prepare');

const model = require('../model/item.js');
const CatalogItem = model.CatalogItem;

mongoose.createConnection('mongodb://localhost/catalog');

describe('CatalogItem: models', function () {
  describe('#create()', function () {
    it('Should create a new CatalogItem', function (done) {
```

```
        var item = {
          "itemId": "1",
          "itemName": "Sports Watch",
          "price": 100,
          "currency": "EUR",
          "categories": [
            "Watches",
            "Sports Watches"
          ]

        };

        CatalogItem.create(item, function (err, createdItem) {
          // Check that no error occured
          should.not.exist(err);
          // Assert that the returned item has is what we expect

          createdItem.itemId.should.equal('1');
          createdItem.itemName.should.equal('Sports Watch');
          createdItem.price.should.equal(100);
          createdItem.currency.should.equal('EUR');
          createdItem.categories[0].should.equal('Watches');
          createdItem.categories[1].should.equal('Sports Watches');
          //Notify mocha that the test has completed
          done();
        });
      });
    });
  });
```

Executing the npm test now results in a call against the MongoDB database creating an item out of the passed JSON object. After insertion, the assert callback will be executing, ensuring that values passed to by Mongoose are the same as the returned ones from the database. Give it a try and break the test—simply change the expected value in the assert with an invalid one—you will see the test failing.

Creating a user-defined model around a Mongoose model

After seeing how a model works, it is time to create a user-defined module that wraps all CRUD operations for the catalog. Since we intend to use that module in a RESTful web application, it seems logical to leave the schema definition and the model creation outside the module and have them provided as arguments of each module function. The same schema definition is used in the unit tests, ensuring stability of the module. Now let's add an implementation for each CRUD function, starting with a `remove()` function. It looks up an item based on its `id` and deletes it from the database, if it exists:

```
exports.remove = function (request, response) {
  console.log('Deleting item with id: '    + request.body.itemId);
  CatalogItem.findOne({itemId: request.params.itemId}, function(error,
data) {
      if (error) {
          console.log(error);
          if (response != null) {
              response.writeHead(500, contentTypePlainText);
              response.end('Internal server error');
          }
          return;
      } else {
          if (!data) {
              console.log('Item not found');
              if (response != null) {
                  response.writeHead(404, contentTypePlainText);
                  response.end('Not Found');
              }
              return;
          } else {
              data.remove(function(error){
                  if (!error) {
                      data.remove();
                      response.json({'Status': 'Successfully deleted'});
                  }
                  else {
                      console.log(error);
                      response.writeHead(500, contentTypePlainText);
                      response.end('Internal Server Error');
                  }
              });
          }
```

```
        }
    });
}
```

The `saveItem()` function takes the request body payload as an argument. A valid update request will contain the new state of an `item` object, represented in JSON format. First, the `itemId` is parsed out of the JSON object. Next, lookup is done. If an item exists, it gets updated. Otherwise, a new one gets created:

```
exports.saveItem = function(request, response)
{
  var item = toItem(request.body);
  item.save((error) => {
    if (!error) {
      item.save();
      response.writeHead(201, contentTypeJson);
      response.end(JSON.stringify(request.body));
    } else {
      console.log(error);
      CatalogItem.findOne({itemId : item.itemId    },
      (error, result) => {
        console.log('Check if such an item exists');
            if (error) {
                console.log(error);
                response.writeHead(500, contentTypePlainText);
                response.end('Internal Server Error');
            } else {
                if (!result) {
                    console.log('Item does not exist. Creating a new one');
                    item.save();
                    response.writeHead(201, contentTypeJson);
                    response.
                    response.end(JSON.stringify(request.body));
                } else {
                    console.log('Updating existing item');
                    result.itemId = item.itemId;
                    result.itemName = item.itemName;
                    result.price = item.price;
                    result.currency = item.currency;
                    result.categories = item.categories;
                    result.save();
                    response.json(JSON.stringify(result));
                }
            }
        }
    });
```

```
      }
   });
};
```

The `toItem()` function converts the JSON payload to a `CatalogItem` model instance, that is, an item document:

```
function toItem(body) {
    return new CatalogItem({
        itemId: body.itemId,
        itemName: body.itemName,
        price: body.price,
        currency: body.currency,
        categories: body.categories
    });
}
```

We will also need to provide a means of querying data, so let's implement a function that queries for all items in a category:

```
exports.findItemsByCategory = function (category, response) {
    CatalogItem.find({categories: category}, function(error, result) {
        if (error) {
            console.error(error);
            response.writeHead(500, { 'Content-Type': 'text/plain' });
            return;
        } else {
            if (!result) {
                if (response != null) {
                    response.writeHead(404, contentTypePlainText);
                    response.end('Not Found');
                }
                return;
            }

            if (response != null){
                response.setHeader('Content-Type', 'application/json');
                response.send(result);
            }
            console.log(result);
        }
    });
}
```

Similar to `findItemsByCategory`, the following is a function that finds an item by its ID:

```
exports.findItemById = function (itemId, response) {
    CatalogItem.findOne({itemId: itemId}, function(error, result) {
        if (error) {
            console.error(error);
            response.writeHead(500, contentTypePlainText);
            return;
        } else {
            if (!result) {
                if (response != null) {
                    response.writeHead(404, contentTypePlainText);
                    response.end('Not Found');
                }
                return;
            }

            if (response != null){
                response.setHeader('Content-Type', 'application/json');
                response.send(result);
            }
            console.log(result);
        }
    });
}
```

Finally, there's a function that lists all the catalog items stored in the database. It uses the Mongoose model `find` function that looks for all documents of the model, and uses its first arguments as a filter. We want a function that returns all existing documents; that's why we provide an empty object. This will return all available items. The results are available in the `callback` function, which is the second argument of the model's `find` function:

```
exports.findAllItems = function (response) {
    CatalogItem.find({}, (error, result) => {
        if (error) {
            console.error(error);
            return null;
        }
        if (result != null) {
            response.json(result);
        } else {
            response.json({});
        }
    });
};
```

The `catalog` module will be the foundation of our RESTful service. It is responsible for all data manipulation operations, as well as for different kinds of queries. It encapsulates all operations in a reusable way.

Wiring up a NoSQL database module to Express

Now we have automated tests for the model and a user-defined module which makes use of them. This ensures the stability of the module and makes it ready for wider adoption.

It is time to build a new Express-based application and add a route, exposing the new module to it:

```
const express = require('express');
const router = express.Router();

const catalog = require('../modules/catalog');
const model = require('../model/item.js');

router.get('/', function(request, response, next) {
  catalog.findAllItems(response);
});

router.get('/item/:itemId', function(request, response, next) {
  console.log(request.url + ' : querying for ' + request.params.itemId);
  catalog.findItemById(request.params.itemId, response);
});

router.get('/:categoryId', function(request, response, next) {
  console.log(request.url + ' : querying for ' +
request.params.categoryId);
  catalog.findItemsByCategory(request.params.categoryId, response);
});

router.post('/', function(request, response, next) {
  console.log('Saving item using POST method);
  catalog.saveItem(request, response);
});

router.put('/', function(request, response, next) {
  console.log('Saving item using PUT method');
  catalog.saveItem(request, response);
});
```

```
router.delete('/item/:itemId', function(request, response, next) {
  console.log('Deleting item with id: request.params.itemId);
  catalog.remove(request, response);
});

module.exports = router;
```

To sum up, we routed each function of the catalog data service module to an operation of a RESTful service:

- GET /catalog/item/:itemId: **This calls** catalog.findItemById()
- POST /catalog: **This calls** catalog.saveItem()
- PUT /catalog: **This calls** catalog.saveItem()
- DELETE / catalog/item/:id: **This calls** catalog.remove()
- GET /catalog/:category: **This calls** catalog.findItemsByCategory()
- GET /catalog/: **This calls** catalog.findAllItems()

As we have our operations exposed, we are ready to perform some more serious REST testing. Let's start Postman and test the newly exposed endpoints:

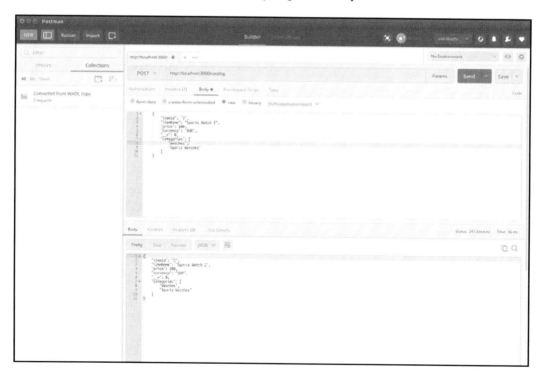

Spend some time testing each operation thoroughly. This will help you gain confidence that the catalog data service module really works, and also will make you more comfortable with how HTTP responses are served and read. As a RESTful API developer, you should be able to read HTTP dumps, which show different request payloads and status codes, fluently.

Self-test questions

Go through the following questions:

- How would you perform a query with Mongoose for a single value of a multivalued attribute?
- Define a strategy for testing a Node.js module manipulating a NoSQL database.

Summary

In this chapter, we looked at MongoDB, a powerful document-oriented database. We utilized it and made use of Mocha to implement an automated test for the database layer. Now it is time to build a fully-fledged RESTful web service. In the next chapter, we will extend the user-defined module by including support for searching via document attributes, and add filtering and pagination capabilities that will finally evolve into full-fledged RESTful service implementation.

5
Restful API Design Guidelines

In the previous chapter, we implemented a catalog module that exposed functions for data manipulation for the items in the catalog application. These functions made use of the `express.js` **request** object to parse the incoming data in the body and then to carry out the appropriate database operation. Each function populated the **response** object with a relevant status code and response body payload, if needed. Finally, we bound each function to a route, accepting HTTP requests.

Now, it's time to look closer into the URLs of the routes and into the returned HTTP status codes per operation.

In this chapter, we will cover the following topics:

- Endpoint URLs and HTTP status codes best practices
- Extensibility and versioning
- Linked data

Endpoint URLs and HTTP status codes best practices

Each RESTful API operation is a combination of an HTTP request against a URL and an appropriate HTTP method.

When executed, each operation will return a status code, indicating whether the invocation has been successful or not. Successful invocation is indicated by a HTTP 2XX status code, while operations that are not executed correctly indicate this with erroneous status code—4XX if the error is at client side, or 5xx when the server fails to process a valid request.

Having a well-specified API is vital for its adoption. Such specification should not only completely enumerate the status codes of each operation, but should also specify the expected data format, that is, its supported media types.

The following table defines how the Express.js Router will expose the API operations, and it should serve as a reference specification for it:

Method	URI	Media type	Description	Status Code
GET	/catalog	application/json	Returns all the items in the catalog.	200 OK 500 Internal Server Error
GET	/catalog/{categoryId}	application/json	Returns all items for the selected category. If the category does not exist, it returns 404.	200 OK, 404 NOT FOUND 500 Internal Server Error
GET	/item/{itemId}	application/json	Returns a single item for the selected itemId. If there is no such item, it returns 404.	200 OK, 404 NOT FOUND 500 Internal Server Error
POST	/item/	application/json	Creates a new item; if an item with the same identifier exists, it will be updated. When an item is created, a **Location** header is returned. It provides the URL where the newly created item can be accessed.	201 Created 200 OK 500 Internal Server Error

PUT	/item/{itemId}	application/json	Updates an existing item; if an item with the provided identifier does not exist, it creates it. When an item is created, a **Location** header is returned. It provides the URL where the newly created item can be accessed.	201 Created 200 OK 500 Internal Server Error
DELETE	/item/{itemId}	application/json	Deletes an existing item; if an item with the provided identifier does not exist, it returns 404.	200 OK, 404 NOT FOUND 500 Internal Server Error

The catalog application handles two types of entities: items and categories. Each item entity contains a collection of categories where it belongs. As you can see, the category is just a logical entity in our application; it will exist as long as there is at least one item referencing it, and will cease to exist when no items refer it. This is why the application exposes routes for exposing data manipulation functions only for resources of type items, while the operations for categories are more or less read only. Looking more carefully into the URLs exposing the data manipulation operations for the items, we can see a clear pattern aligning the URL to the REST fundamental principles—a resource is exposed by a single URL, and it supports resource manipulation actions that are determined by the HTTP method of the request. To sum up, listed here are the generally accepted rules that a well-defined API should follow. They are semantically related to each resource manipulation operation:

- When a **new** resource is created, the service makes use of the **201 Created** status code, followed by a location header that specifies the URL where the newly created resource can be accessed.
- Operation that creates resources may be implemented to gracefully reject creation of resources, which unique identifiers already use; in such cases, the operation should indicate a non-successful invocation with an appropriate status code **409 Conflict**, or a more general **400 BAD REQUEST**. However, a general status code should always be followed by a meaningful explanation of what has gone wrong. In our implementation, we choose a different approach—we update the resource from the create operation, if it exists, and notify the caller that the resource was updated by returning the **200 OK** status code instead of **201 Created**.

- The **Update** operation resembles the create operation; however, it always expects a resource identifier as a parameter, if a resource with this identifier exists—it gets updated with a new state provided in the body of the HTTP PUT request. The **200 OK** status code indicates successful invocation. The implementation may decide to reject handling of non-existent resources with the **404 Not Found** status code or creating a new resource with the passed identifier. In that case, it would return the **201 Created** status code, followed by a location header that specifies the URL where the newly created resource can be accessed. Our API makes use of the second option.

- While successful **deletion** can be indicated with the **204 No Content** status and further payload, most user agents would expect the **2xx** HTTP status to be followed by a body. Thus, to stay compatible with most of the agents, our API will indicate successful deletion with the **200 OK** status code, followed by a JSON payload:`{'Status': 'Successfully deleted'}`. Status code **404 Not found** will indicate that a resource with the provided identifier does not exist.

- As a general rule, **5XX** should not indicate application state errors but more severe errors, such as application server or database failures.

- It is best practice that `update` and `create` operations should return as a payload to the entire state of the resource. For instance, if a resource is created with a minimum set of attributes, all non specified attribute will get default values; the response body should contain the full state of the object. The same is valid for updates; even if an update operation updates the resource restate partially, the response should return the complete state. This may save the user-agent an additional GET request if they needed to check the new state.

Now that we have defined some general recommendations on how operations should behave, it's time to implement them in a new version of the API.

Extensibility and versioning

We've already defined a few basic versioning rules in `Chapter 3`, *Building a Typical Web API*. Let's apply them to the MongoDB database-aware module we implemented in the previous chapter. Our starting point would be to enable the current consumers of the API to continue using the same version on a different URL. This will keep them backward-compatible until they adopt and successfully test the new version.

Keeping a REST API stable is not a question of only moving one endpoint from one URI to another. It makes no sense to perform redirection and afterward have an API that behaves differently. Thus, we need to ensure that the behavior of the moved endpoint stays the same. To ensure that we don't change the previously implemented behavior, let's move the current behavior from the `catalog.js` module to a new module by renaming the file to `catalogV1.js`. Then, make a copy of it to the `catalogV2.js` module, where we will introduce all new functionality; but before doing that, we have to reroute Version 1 from `/`, `/{categoryId}`, `/{itemId}` to `/v1`, `/v1/{categoryId}`, `/v1/{itemId}`:

```javascript
const express = require('express');
const router = express.Router();

const catalogV1 = require('../modules/catalogV1');
const model = require('../model/item.js');

router.get('/v1/', function(request, response, next) {
  catalogV1.findAllItems(response);
});

router.get('/v1/item/:itemId', function(request, response, next) {
  console.log(request.url + ' : querying for ' + request.params.itemId);
  catalogV1.findItemById(request.params.itemId, response);
});

router.get('/v1/:categoryId', function(request, response, next) {
  console.log(request.url + ' : querying for ' +
request.params.categoryId);
  catalogV1.findItemsByCategory(request.params.categoryId, response);
});

router.post('/v1/', function(request, response, next) {
  catalogV1.saveItem(request, response);
});

router.put('/v1/', function(request, response, next) {
  catalogV1.saveItem(request, response);
});

router.delete('/v1/item/:itemId', function(request, response, next) {
  catalogV1.remove(request, response);
});

router.get('/', function(request, response) {
  console.log('Redirecting to v1');
  response.writeHead(301, {'Location' : '/catalog/v1/'});
  response.end('Version 1 is moved to /catalog/v1/: ');
```

```
});

module.exports = router;
```

Since Version 2 of our API is not yet implemented, executing a GET request against / will result in receiving a 301 Moved Permanently HTTP status, which will then redirect to /v1/. This will notify our consumers that the API is evolving and that they will soon need to decide whether to continue using Version 1 by explicitly requesting its new URI or prepare for adopting Version 2.

Go ahead and give it a try! Start the modified node application and, from Postman, make a GET request to http://localhost:3000/catalog:

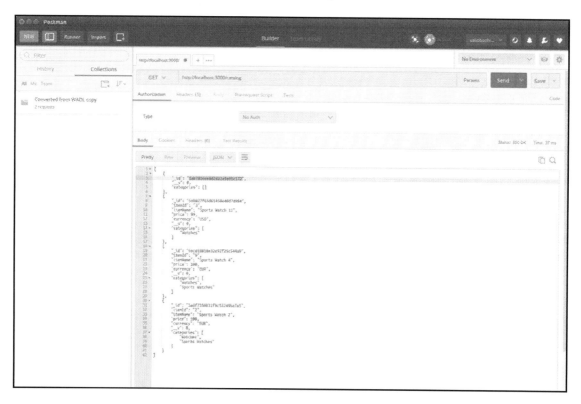

You will see that your request is redirected to the newly routed location at http://localhost:3000/catalog/v1.

Now that we have finalized Version 1 of the catalog, it's time to think of further extensions that we can add in Version 2. Currently, the catalog service supports listing of all items in a category and fetching an item by its ID. It's about time to take full advantage of MongoDB, being a document-oriented database, and implement a function that will enable our API consumer to query for items based on any of their attributes. For instance, list all items for a specific category with an attribute that matches a query parameter, such as price or color, or search by item name. RESTful services usually expose document-oriented data. However, their usage is not limited to documents only. In the next chapter, we will extend the catalog in a way that it also stores binary data—an image that can be linked to each item. For that purpose, we will use a MongoDB binary format called **Binary JSON (BSON)** in the *Working with arbitrary data* section in Chapter 6, *Implementing a Full-Fledged RESTful Service*.

Getting back to the searching extension, we've already used the Mongoose.js model's find() and findOne() functions. So far, we used them to provide the name of the document attribute to be searched with, statically, in our JavaScript code. However, this filtering parameter of find() is just a JSON object where the key is the document attribute and the value is the attribute's value to be used in the query. Here is the first new function we will add to Version 2. It queries MongoDB by an arbitrary attribute and its value:

```
exports.findItemsByAttribute = function (key, value, response) {
    var filter = {};
    filter[key] = value;
    CatalogItem.find(filter, function(error, result) {
        if (error) {
            console.error(error);
            response.writeHead(500, contentTypePlainText);
            response.end('Internal server error');
            return;
        } else {
            if (!result) {
                if (response != null) {
                    response.writeHead(200, contentTypeJson);
                    response.end({});
                }
                return;
            }
            if (response != null){
                response.setHeader('Content-Type', 'application/json');
                response.send(result);
            }
        }
    });
}
```

This function calls find on the model with the provided attribute and value as parameters. We will bind this function to the router's /v2/item/ GET handler.

At the end, our aim is to have /v2/item/?currency=USD that returns only records for items that are sold in USD currency, as indicated by the value of the passed GET parameter. That way, if we modify the model with additional attributes, such as color and size, we can query for all items having the same color or any other attribute that an item can have.

We will keep the old behavior of returning a list of all available items when no parameters are provided within the query string, but we will also parse the query string for the first provided GET parameter and use it as a filter in the findItemsByAttribute() function:

```
router.get('/v2/items', function(request, response) {
    var getParams = url.parse(request.url, true).query;
    if (Object.keys(getParams).length == 0) {
      catalogV2.findAllItems(response);
    } else {
      var key = Object.keys(getParams)[0];
      var value = getParams[key];
      catalogV2.findItemsByAttribute(key, value, response);
    }
});
```

Perhaps the most interesting part in this function is the URL parsing. As you can see, we keep using the same old strategy to check whether any GET parameters are supplied. We parse the URL in order to get the query string, and then we use the built-in Object.keys function to check whether the parsed key/value list contains elements. If it does, we take the first element and extract its value. Both the key and the value are passed to the findByAttribute function.

You may want to improve Version 2 further by providing search support by multiple arguments that are provided by more than one GET parameters. I will leave that to you as an exercise.

Linked data

Every catalog application supports an image or set of images bound to this item. For that purpose, in the next chapter, we will see how to work with binary objects in MongoDB. However, now is the time to decide how to semantically link the binary data to an item document. Extending the model schema in such a way that it contains binary base64 representation of binary data in the document is anything but a good idea, as mixing literally encoded and binary data in one format is never a good idea. It increases the complexity of the application and makes it error-prone:

```
{
  "_id": "5a4c004b0eed73835833cc9a",
  "itemId": "1",
  "itemName": "Sports Watch",
  "price": 100,
  "currency": "EUR",
  "categories": [
    "Watches",
    "Sports Watches"
  ],
  "image":"
```
iVBORw0KGgoAAAANSUhEUgAAAJEAAACRCAMAAAD0BqoRAAAAGXRFWHRTb2Z0d2FyZQBBZG9iZSB
JbWFnZVJlYWR5ccllPAAAAyJpVFh0WE1OMmNvbS5hZG9iZS54bXAAAAAAADw/eHBhY2tldCBiZW
dpbj0i77u/IiBpZD0iVzVNME1wQ2VoaUh6cmVTek5UY3prYzlkIj8+IDx4OnhtcG1ldGEgeG1sb
nM6eD0iYWRvYmU6bnM6bWV0YS8iIHg6eG1wdGs9IkFkb2JlIFhNUCBDb3JlIDUuMC1jMDYwIDYx
LjEzNDc3Nywgy4yMDAxMC8wMi8xMi0xNzozMjowMCAgICAgICAgICI+PHJkZjpSREYgeG1sbnM6cmR
mPSJodHRwOi8vd3d3LnczLm9yZy8xOTk5LzAyLzIyLXJkZi1zeW50YXgtbnMjIj4gPHJkZjpEZXX
NuzjcmlwdGlvbiByZGY6YWJvdXQ9IiIgeG1sbnM6eG1wPSJodHRwOi8vbnMuYWRvYmUuY29tL3h
hcC8xLjAvIiB4bWxuczp4bXBNTT0iaHR0cDovL25zLmFkb2JlLmNvbS94YXAvMS4wL21tLyIgeG
1sbnM6c3RSZWY9Imh0dHA6Ly9ucy5hZG9iZS5jb20veGFwLzEuMC9zVHlwZS9SZXNvdXJjZVJlZ
iMiIHhtcDpDcmVhdG9yVG9vbD0iQWRvYmUgUGhvdG9zaG9wIENTNSBNYWNpbnRvc2giIHhtcE1N
Okluc3RhbmNlSUQ9InhtcC5paWQ6MjMwNjQ1NDddFNjJCMTFFRkkI5QzU4OTFCMjJCQzEzM0EiIHh
tcE1NOkRvY3VtZW50SUQ9InhtcC5kaWQ6MjMwNjQ1NDhFNjJCMTFFRkkI5QzU4OTFCMjJCQzEzM0
EiPiA8eG1wTU06RGVyaXZlZEZyb20gc3RSZWY6aW5zdGFuY2VJRD0ieG1wLmlpZDoyMzA2NDU0N
UU2MkIxMURGQGjlDNTg5MUIyMkJDMTMzQSIgc3RSZWY6ZG9jdW1lbnRJRD0ieG1wLmRpZDoyMzA2
NDU0NkU2MkIxMURGQGjlDNTg5MUIyMkJDMTMzQSIvPiA8L3JkZjpEZXNjcmlwdGlvbj4gPC9yZGY
6UkRGPiA8L3g6eG1wbWV0YT4gPD94cGFja2V0IGVuZD0iciI/Px5Xq1XXhWFY1+v151/b3ij5tI
/GPEVP0e8U/SPAABPLjHnaJ6XvAAAAElFTkSuQmCC
```
"}
```

Imagine how large a result for a non-filtered query can become just for a few hundred items, if all of them had an image binary representation as a value of a JSON attribute. To avoid that, we will return the image for each item at a URL that is logically linked to the resource's URL—`/catalog/v2/item/{itemId}/image`.

That way, if there is an image assigned to an item, it will be served at a known location. This approach, however, does not semantically link the binary item to its corresponding resource, as when accessing the item at `/catalog/v2/item/{itemId}`, there would be no indication of whether it has an image assigned or not. To solve this, let's use a custom HTTP header in response of the item route:

```
GET http://localhost:3000/catalog/v2/item/1 HTTP/1.1
Host: localhost:3000
Connection: Keep-Alive
User-Agent: Apache-HttpClient/4.1.1 (java 1.5)

HTTP/1.1 200 OK
X-Powered-By: Express
Content-Type: application/json; charset=utf-8
Content-Length: 152
Image-Url: http://localhost:3000/catalog/v2/item/1/image
ETag: W/"98-2nJj2mZdLV2YDME3WYCyEwIXfuA"
Date: Thu, 01 Feb 2018 13:50:43 GMT
Connection: keep-alive

{
  "_id": "5a4c004b0eed73835833cc9a",
  "itemId": "1",
  "itemName": "Sports Watch",
  "price": 100,
  "currency": "EUR",
  "__v": 0,
  "categories": [
    "Watches",
    "Sports Watches"
  ]
}
```

When present in the response, the `Image-Url` header indicates that the item has an additional resource bound to it, and the header value provides the address where it is available. Using this approach, we linked a binary resource semantically to our document.

In the next chapter, we will implement the routes that will handle the manipulation of arbitrary items bound to the items in the catalog.

Summary

In this chapter, we discussed in detail how resources should be exposed via a RESTful API; we paid close attention to URL best practices and looked into appropriate usage of the HTTP status codes indicating each state of our operations.

We covered the topics of versioning and extensibility, where we used the `301 Moved Permanently` status code to automatically redirect API calls to different URLs.

Finally, we figured out how to semantically link our resource items to arbitrary binary represented data.

6
Implementing a Full Fledged RESTful Service

So far, we have created a second version of our RESTful service, and we had the two versions exposed by different URLs, ensuring backward compatibility. We implemented unit tests for its database layer and discussed how to use HTTP status codes appropriately. In this chapter, we will extend that implementation—by providing handling of non-document—binary data to the second version of the service and linking it accordingly to the documents it relates to.

We will look at a convenient way of presenting large result sets to consumers. For that purpose, we will introduce pagination as well as further filtering capabilities to our API.

There are cases when caching data responses should be considered as an option. We will look at its benefits and drawbacks and also decide to enable caching when necessary.

Finally, we will dive into the discovery and exploration of REST services.

To sum up, here's what should be further implemented to turn the catalog data service into a full-fledged RESTful service:

- Working with arbitrary data
- Working with Linked data in the real world
- Paging and filtering
- Caching
- Discovery and exploration

Working with arbitrary data

MongoDB utilizes BSON (Binary JSON) as the primary data format. It is a binary format that stores key/value pairs in a single entity called **document.** For example, a sample JSON, `{"hello":"world"}`, becomes
`\x16\x00\x00\x00\x02hello\x00\x06\x00\x00\x00world\x00\x00` when encoded in BSON.

BSON stores data rather than literals. For instance, if an image is to be part of the document, it will not have to be converted to a base64-encoded string; instead, it will be directly stored as binary data, unlike plain JSON, which will usually represent such data as base64-encoded bytes, but that is obviously not the most efficient way.

Mongoose schemas enable storing binary content in the BSON format via the schema type—**buffer.** It stores binary content (image, ZIP archive, and so on) up to 16 MB. The reason behind the relatively small storage capacity is to prevent excessive usage of memory and bandwidth during transmission.

The **GridFS** specification addresses this limitation of BSON and enables you to work with data larger than 16 MB. GridFS divides data into chunks stored as separate document entries. Each chunk, by default, has a size of up to 255 KB. When data is requested from the data store, the GridFS driver retrieves all the required chunks and returns them in an assembled order, as if they had never been divided. Not only does this mechanism allow storage of data larger than 16 MB, it also enables consumers to retrieve data in portions so that it doesn't have to be loaded completely into the memory. Thus, the specification implicitly enables streaming support.

GridFS actually offers more—it supports storing metadata for the given binary data, for example, its format, a filename, size, and so on. The metadata is stored in a separate file and is available for more complex queries. There is a very usable Node.js module called `gridfs-stream`. It enables easy streaming of data in and out of MongoDB, as on all other modules it is installed as an `npm` package. So, let's install it globally and see how it is used; we will also use the `-s` option to ensure that the dependencies in the project's `package.json` are updated:

```
npm install -g -s gridfs-stream
```

To create a `Grid` instance, you are required to have a connection opened to the database:

```
const mongoose = require('mongoose')
const Grid = require('gridfs-stream');

mongoose.connect('mongodb://localhost/catalog');
var connection = mongoose.connection;
var gfs = Grid(connection.db, mongoose.mongo);
```

Reading and writing into the stream is done through the `createReadStream()` and `createWriteStream()` functions. Each piece of data streamed into the database must have an `ObjectId` attribute set. The `ObjectId` identifies binary data entry uniquely, just as it would have identified any other document in MongoDB; using this `ObjectId`, we can find or delete it from the MongoDB collection by this identifier.

Let's extend the catalog service with functions for fetching, adding, and deleting an image assigned to an item. For simplicity, the service will support a single image per item, so there will be a single function responsible for adding an image. It will overwrite an existing image each time it is invoked, so an appropriate name for it is `saveImage`:

```
exports.saveImage = function(gfs, request, response) {

    var writeStream = gfs.createWriteStream({
            filename : request.params.itemId,
            mode : 'w'
    });

    writeStream.on('error', function(error) {
        response.send('500', 'Internal Server Error');
        console.log(error);
        return;
    })

    writeStream.on('close', function() {
        readImage(gfs, request, response);
    });

    request.pipe(writeStream);
}
```

As you can see, all we need to do to flush the data in MongoDB is to create a GridFS write stream instance. It requires some options that provide the `ObjectId` of the MongoDB entry and some additional metadata, such as a title as well as the writing mode. Then, we simply call the pipe function of the request. Piping will result in flushing the data from the request to the write stream, and, in this way, it will be safely stored in MongoDB. Once stored, the `close` event associated with the `writeStream` will occur, and this is when our function reads back whatever it has stored in the database and returns that image in the HTTP response.

Retrieving an image is done the other way around—a `readStream` is created with options, and the value of the `_id` parameter should be the `ObjectId` of the arbitrary data, optional file name, and read mode:

```
function readImage(gfs, request, response) {

  var imageStream = gfs.createReadStream({
      filename : request.params.itemId,
      mode : 'r'
  });

  imageStream.on('error', function(error) {
    console.log(error);
    response.send('404', 'Not found');
    return;
  });
  response.setHeader('Content-Type', 'image/jpeg');
  imageStream.pipe(response);
}
```

Before piping the read stream to the response, the appropriate `Content-Type` header has to be set so that the arbitrary data can be presented to the client with an appropriate image media type, `image/jpeg`, in our case.

Finally, we export from our module a function for fetching the image back from MongoDB. We will use that function to bind it to the express route that reads the image from the database:

```
exports.getImage = function(gfs, itemId, response) {
    readImage(gfs, itemId, response);
};
```

Deleting arbitrary data from MongoDB is also straightforward. You have to delete the entry from two internal MongoDB collections, the `fs.files`, where all the files are kept, and from the `fs.files.chunks`:

```
exports.deleteImage = function(gfs, mongodb, itemId, response) {
    console.log('Deleting image for itemId:' + itemId);

    var options = {
            filename : itemId,
    };

    var chunks = mongodb.collection('fs.files.chunks');
    chunks.remove(options, function (error, image) {
        if (error) {
            console.log(error);
            response.send('500', 'Internal Server Error');
            return;
        } else {
            console.log('Successfully deleted image for item: ' + itemId);
        }
    });

    var files = mongodb.collection('fs.files');
    files.remove(options, function (error, image) {
        if (error) {
            console.log(error);
            response.send('500', 'Internal Server Error');
            return;
        }

        if (image === null) {
            response.send('404', 'Not found');
            return;
        } else {
            console.log('Successfully deleted image for primary item: ' +
itemId);
            response.json({'deleted': true});
        }
    });
}
```

Let's bind the new functionality to the appropriate item route and test it:

```
router.get('/v2/item/:itemId/image',
  function(request, response){
    var gfs = Grid(model.connection.db, mongoose.mongo);
    catalogV2.getImage(gfs, request, response);
});

router.get('/item/:itemId/image',
  function(request, response){
    var gfs = Grid(model.connection.db, mongoose.mongo);
    catalogV2.getImage(gfs, request, response);
});

router.post('/v2/item/:itemId/image',
  function(request, response){
    var gfs = Grid(model.connection.db, mongoose.mongo);
    catalogV2.saveImage(gfs, request, response);
});

router.post('/item/:itemId/image',
  function(request, response){
    var gfs = Grid(model.connection.db, mongoose.mongo);
    catalogV2.saveImage(gfs, request.params.itemId, response);
});

router.put('/v2/item/:itemId/image',
  function(request, response){
    var gfs = Grid(model.connection.db, mongoose.mongo);
    catalogV2.saveImage (gfs, request.params.itemId, response);
});

router.put('/item/:itemId/image',
function(request, response){
  var gfs = Grid(model.connection.db, mongoose.mongo);
  catalogV2.saveImage(gfs, request.params.itemId, response);
});

router.delete('/v2/item/:itemId/image',
function(request, response){
  var gfs = Grid(model.connection.db, mongoose.mongo);
  catalogV2.deleteImage(gfs, model.connection,
  request.params.itemId, response);
});

router.delete('/item/:itemId/image',
function(request, response){
  var gfs = Grid(model.connection.db, mongoose.mongo);
```

```
catalogV2.deleteImage(gfs, model.connection,  request.params.itemId,
response);
});
```

 Since, at the time of writing, Version 2 is the latest version of our API, any new functionality exposed by it should be available at both locations: `/catalog` and `/v2/catalog`.

Let's start Postman and post an image to an existing item, assuming that we have an item with ID 14 `/catalog/v2/item/14/image`:

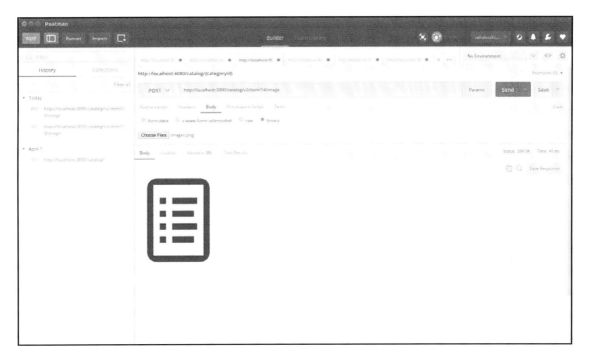

Post request assigning an image to an item using Postman. This is a screenshot for Postman. The individual settings are not important here. The purpose of the image is just to show how the window looks.

After the request is processed, the binary data is stored in the grid datastore and the image is returned in the response.

Linking

In the Linked data section of the previous chapter, we defined that if an item in the catalog has an image assigned to it, this will be indicated with an HTTP header named **Image-URL**.

Let's modify the `findItemById` function in the V2 of the catalog. We will use the GridFS's existing function to check whether there is an image bound to the selected item; in case there is an image assigned to the item, its URL will be available to the response with the Image-Url header:

```
exports.findItemById = function (gfs, request, response) {
    CatalogItem.findOne({itemId: request.params.itemId}, function(error,
result) {
        if (error) {
            console.error(error);
            response.writeHead(500,     contentTypePlainText);
            return;
        } else {
            if (!result) {
                if (response != null) {
                    response.writeHead(404, contentTypePlainText);
                    response.end('Not Found');
                }
                return;
            }

            var options = {
                filename : result.itemId,
            };
            gfs.exist(options, function(error, found) {
                if (found) {
                    response.setHeader('Content-Type', 'application/json');
                    var imageUrl = request.protocol + '://' +
request.get('host') + request.baseUrl + request.path + '/image';
                    response.setHeader('Image-Url', imageUrl);
                    response.send(result);
                } else {
                    response.json(result);
                }
            });
        }
    });
}
```

So far, we linked an item to its image; however, that leaves our data partially linked, as there is a link from an item to its image but not the other way around. Let's change that and supply a header Item-Url to the image response by modifying the `readImage` function:

```
function readImage(gfs, request, response) {

  var imageStream = gfs.createReadStream({
      filename : request.params.itemId,
      mode : 'r'
  });

  imageStream.on('error', function(error) {
    console.log(error);
    response.send('404', 'Not found');
    return;
  });

  var itemImageUrl = request.protocol + '://' + request.get('host') +
request.baseUrl+ request.path;
  var itemUrl = itemImageUrl.substring(0, itemImageUrl.indexOf('/image'));
  response.setHeader('Content-Type', 'image/jpeg');
  response.setHeader('Item-Url', itemUrl);

  imageStream.pipe(response);
}
```

Now requesting the item at `http://localhost:3000/catalog/v2/item/3/` will return the item encoded in the JSON format:

```
GET http://localhost:3000/catalog/v2/item/3/image HTTP/1.1
Accept-Encoding: gzip,deflate
Host: localhost:3000

HTTP/1.1 200 OK
X-Powered-By: Express
Content-Type: application/json; charset=utf-8
Image-Url: http://localhost:3000/catalog/v2/item/3/image
Content-Length: 137
Date: Tue, 03 Apr 2018 19:47:41 GMT
Connection: keep-alive

{
    "_id": "5ab827f65d61450e40d7d984",
    "itemId": "3",
    "itemName": "Sports Watch 11",
    "price": 99,
    "currency": "USD",
```

```
      "__v": 0,
      "categories": ["Watches"]
  }
```

Looking into the response headers, we find the `Image-Url` header its value, `http://localhost:3000/catalog/v2/item/3/image` provides the URL of the image linked to the item.

Requesting that image results in the following:

```
GET http://localhost:3000/catalog/v2/item/3/image HTTP/1.1
Host: localhost:3000
Connection: Keep-Alive

HTTP/1.1 200 OK
X-Powered-By: Express
Content-Type: image/jpeg
Item-Url: http://localhost:3000/catalog/v2/item/3
Connection: keep-alive
Transfer-Encoding: chunked

<BINARY DATA>
```

This time, the response provides the payload of the image linked to the item and a special header **Item-Url**. Its value—`http://localhost:3000/catalog/v2/item/3`—is the address where the item resource is available. Now if the item image appears, for instance, in image search results, the URL of the item linked with the image will also be part of the result. In this way, we linked the two data semantically without modifying or compromising their payload.

Implementing paging and filtering

Once deployed to the web, each service becomes available to an enormous number of consumers. They will not only use it to get data but also to insert new data. At some point of time, this will inevitably lead to a large amount of data being available in the database. To keep the service user-friendly and maintain a reasonable response time, we need to take care of providing big data in reasonable portions, assuring that it does not need to return a few hundred thousand items when the `/catalog` URI is requested.

Web data consumers are used to having various pagination and filtering capabilities. Earlier in this chapter, we implemented the `findIfindItemsByAttribute()` function, which enabled filtering by any of the attributes of an item Now, it's time to introduce pagination capabilities to enable navigation within the `resultset` with the help of a URI parameter.

The `mongoose.js` models can make use of different plugin modules to provide additional functionality on top of them. Such a plugin module is `mongoose-paginate`. The Express framework also provides a piece of pagination middleware named `express-paginate`. It provides out-of-the-box linking and navigation with Mongoose's result pages:

1. Before starting to develop the pagination mechanism, we should install these two useful modules:

   ```
   npm install -g -s express-paginate
   npm install -g -s mongoose-paginate
   ```

2. The next step will to be to create instances of the `express-paginate` middleware in our application:

   ```
   expressPaginate = require('express-paginate');
   ```

3. Initialize the pagination middleware in the application by calling its `middleware()` function. Its parameters specify a default limit and a maximum limit of results per page:

   ```
   app.use(expressPaginate.middleware(limit, maxLimit));
   ```

4. Then, provide the `mongoose-pagination` instance as a plugin to the `CatalogItem` schema before creating a model. Here's how the `item.js` module will export that along with the model:

   ```
   var mongoose = require('mongoose');
   var mongoosePaginate = require('mongoose-paginate');
   var Schema = mongoose.Schema;

   mongoose.connect('mongodb://localhost/catalog');

   var itemSchema = new Schema ({
       "itemId" : {type: String, index: {unique: true}},
       "itemName": String,
       "price": Number,
       "currency" : String,
       "categories": [String]
   });
   console.log('paginate');
   ```

```
itemSchema.plugin(mongoosePaginate);
var CatalogItem = mongoose.model('Item', itemSchema);

module.exports = {CatalogItem : CatalogItem, connection :
mongoose.connection};
```

5. Finally, call the `paginate()` function of the model to fetch the requested entries in a paginated manner:

```
CatalogItem.paginate({}, {page:request.query.page,
limit:request.query.limit},
    function (error, result){
        if(error) {
            console.log(error);
            response.writeHead('500',
                {'Content-Type' : 'text/plain'});
            response.end('Internal Server Error');
        } else {
            response.json(result);
        }
});
```

The first parameter is the filter that Mongoose should use for its query. The second parameter is an object specifying which page is requested and the entries per page. The third parameter is a callback-handler function, providing the result and any available error information via its parameters:

- `error`: This specifies whether the query was executed successfully
- `result`: This is the retrieved data from the database

The `express-paginate` middleware enables seamless integration of the `mongoose-paginate` module in the web environment by enriching the `request` and `response` objects of an Express handler function.

The `request` objects get two new attributes: `query.limit`, which tells the middleware the number of entries on the page, and `query.page`, which specifies the requested page. Note that the middleware will ignore values of `query.limit` that are larger than the `maxLimit` value specified at the middleware's initialization. This prevents the consumer from overriding the maximum limit and gives you total control over your application.

Here's the implementation of the `paginate` function in the second version of the catalog module:

```
exports.paginate = function(model, request, response) {
    var pageSize = request.query.limit;
```

```
var page = request.query.page;
if (pageSize === undefined) {
    pageSize = 100;
}
if (page === undefined) {
    page = 1;
}

model.paginate({}, {page:page, limit:pageSize},
        function (error, result){
            if(error) {
                console.log(error);
                response.writeHead('500',
                    {'Content-Type' : 'text/plain'});
                response.end('Internal Server Error');
            }
            else {
                response.json(result);
            }
        });
}
```

The following is the response from querying a dataset containing 11 items with a limit of five items per page:

```
{
  "docs": [
    {
      "_id": "5a4c004b0eed73835833cc9a",
      "itemId": "1",
      "itemName": "Sports Watch 1",
      "price": 100,
      "currency": "EUR",
      "__v": 0,
      "categories": [
        "Watches",
        "Sports Watches"
      ]
    },
    {
      "_id": "5a4c0b7aad0ebbce584593ee",
      "itemId": "2",
      "itemName": "Sports Watch 2",
      "price": 100,
      "currency": "USD",
      "__v": 0,
      "categories": [
        "Sports Watches"
```

```
        ]
      },
      {
        "_id": "5a64d7ecfa1b585142008017",
        "itemId": "3",
        "itemName": "Sports Watch 3",
        "price": 100,
        "currency": "USD",
        "__v": 0,
        "categories": [
          "Watches",
          "Sports Watches"
        ]
      },
      {
        "_id": "5a64d9a59f4dc4e34329b80f",
        "itemId": "8",
        "itemName": "Sports Watch 4",
        "price": 100,
        "currency": "EUR",
        "__v": 0,
        "categories": [
          "Watches",
          "Sports Watches"
        ]
      },
      {
        "_id": "5a64da377d25d96e44c9c273",
        "itemId": "9",
        "itemName": "Sports Watch 5",
        "price": 100,
        "currency": "USD",
        "__v": 0,
        "categories": [
          "Watches",
          "Sports Watches"
        ]
      }
    ],
    "total": 11,
    "limit": "5",
    "page": "1",
    "pages": 3
}
```

The `docs` attribute contains all the items that are part of the results. Its size is the same as the selected limit value. The `pages` attribute provides the total number of pages; in the example here, its value is 3, as 11 items are accommodated in three pages, each containing five items. The `Total` attribute gives us the total number of items.

The final step to enable pagination is to modify the `/v2/` route to start making use of the newly created function:

```
router.get('/v2/', function(request, response) {
  var getParams = url.parse(request.url, true).query;
  if (getParams['page'] !=null) {
    catalogV2.paginate(model.CatalogItem, request, response);
  } else {
    var key = Object.keys(getParams)[0];
    var value = getParams[key];
    catalogV2.findItemsByAttribute(key, value, response);
  }
});
```

We will use the HTTP `302 Found` status for the default route, `/catalog`. In this way, all incoming requests will be redirected to `/v2/`:

```
router.get('/', function(request, response) {
  console.log('Redirecting to v2');
  response.writeHead(302, {'Location' : '/catalog/v2/'});
  response.end('Version 2 is is available at /catalog/v2/: ');
});
```

Using an appropriate status code for redirection here is vital to the life cycle of any RESTful web service. Returning `302 Found`, followed by a redirection, ensures that the consumer of the API will always have its latest version available at that location. Furthermore, it is also a good practice from the development point of view to use redirection instead of code duplication here.

When you are between two versions, you should always consider using the HTTP `301 Moved Permanently` status to show where the previous version has been moved and the HTTP `302 Found` status to show the actual URI of the current version.

Now, getting back to pagination, as the requested page and the limit number are provided as `GET` parameters and we don't want to mix that up with the filtering capabilities, there is an explicit check for them. Pagination will be used only when either the page or the limit `GET` parameters, are available in the request. Otherwise, searching will be carried out.

Initially, we set the maximum limit of 100 results and a default limit of 10, so, before trying the new pagination functionality, ensure that you insert more items than the default limit into the database. This will make the test results more obvious.

Now, let's give it a try. Requesting `/catalog?limit=3` will result in returning a list containing only two items, as shown:

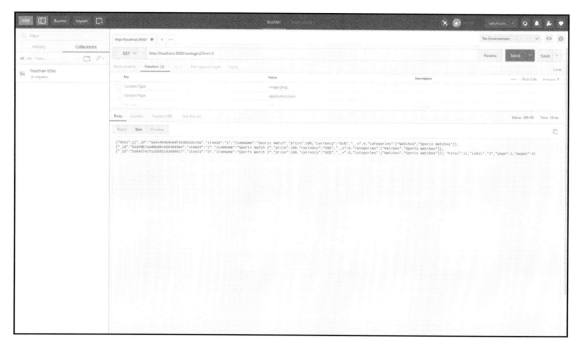

Pagination enabled results. This is a screenshot for Postman. The individual settings are not important here. The purpose of the image is just to show how the window looks.

As you can see from the example, the total number of pages is four. The total number of items is stored in the database 11. Since we didn't specify a page parameter in the request, the pagination implicitly returned the first page. To navigate to the next page, simply add `&page=2` to the URI.

Also, try changing the `limit` attribute, requesting `/catalog/v2?limit=4`. This will return the first four items, and the response will show that the total number of pages is three.

Caching

When we discussed the REST principles defined by Roy Fielding, we mentioned that caching was a rather sensitive topic. In the end, our consumers will expect up-to-date results when executing a query. However, from a statistical point of view, data exposed in the web is more likely to be read rather than updated or deleted.

So, it is reasonable that some resources exposed by a public URL become a subject of millions of requests, considering taking off part of the load from the server to a cache. The HTTP protocol allows us to cache some responses for a given period of time. For instance, when multiple requests are received in a short period of time, querying for all items in the catalog of a given group, such as `/catalog/v2`, our service can utilize special HTTP headers that would force the HTTP server to cache the response for a defined time period. This would prevent redundant requests to the underlying database server.

Caching at the HTTP server level is achieved via special response headers. The HTTP server uses a `Cache-Control` header to specify how long a given response should be cached for. The period before the cache needs invalidation is set via its `max-age` attribute, and its value is provided in seconds. Of course, there is a nice Node.js module that provides a middleware function for caching, called `express-cache-control`.

Supplying the Cache-Control header in Express applications

Let's install it with the NPM package manager; once again, we will install it globally and make use of the `-s` option, which will update the `package.json` file with the new `express-cache-control` dependency automatically:

```
npm install -g -s express-cache-control
```

Enabling caching with the `express-cache-control` middleware requires three straightforward steps:

1. Get the module:

```
CacheControl = require("express-cache-control")
```

2. Create an instance of the `CacheControl` middleware:

```
var cache = new CacheControl().middleware;
```

3. To bind the middleware instance to the routes you want to enable caching for:

```
router.get('/v2/', cache('minutes', 1), function(request, response)
{
    var getParams = url.parse(request.url, true).query;
    if (getParams['page'] !=null || getParams['limit'] != null) {
      catalogV2.paginate(model.CatalogItem, request, response);
    } else {
      var key = Object.keys(getParams)[0];
      var value = getParams[key];
      catalogV2.findItemsByAttribute(key, value, response);
    }
});
```

 Usually, common URIs that provide many result entries should be the subject of caching, rather than URIs providing data for a concrete entry. In our application, only the /catalog URI will make use of caching. The max-age attribute must be selected according to the load of your application to minimize inaccurate responses.

Let's test our changes by requesting /catalog/v2 in Postman:

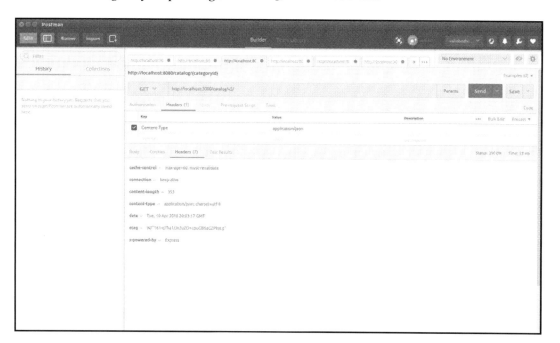

Cache-control header indicating that caching is enabled. This is a screenshot for Postman. The individual settings are not important here. The purpose of the image is just to show how the window looks.

As expected, the `express-cache-control` middleware has done its job—the `Cache-Control` header is now included in the response. The `must-revalidate` option ensures that the cache content is invalidated after the `max-age` interval expires. Now, if you make another request for a specific item, you will see that the response does not make use of the `express-cache-control` middleware, which is because it needs to be explicitly provided in each individual route. It will not be used in URIs deriving from one another.

Responses from `GET` requests against any route `/v1/` will not contain the `Cache-Control` header, as it is supported only in Version 2 of our API, and the `Cache-Control` middleware is used only in the main catalog routes: `/catalog/v2/` or `/catalog`.

Discovering and exploring RESTful services

The topic of discovering RESTful services has a long and complicated history. The HTTP specification states that a resource should be self-descriptive and that it should be identified uniquely by a URI. Dependent resources should be linked by the dependency using their own unique URIs. Discovering a RESTful service means navigating from one service to another, following the links it provides.

In the year 2009, a specification called **Web Application Discovery Language** (**WADL**) was invented. It aims to document every URI exposed from a web application, along with the HTTP methods it supports and the parameter it expects. The response media type of the URI is also described. This is very useful for documenting purposes, and it's all that a WADL file can provide us in terms of RESTful service provisioning.

Unfortunately, there is currently no Node.js module that can automatically generate a WADL file for a given express route. We will have to manually create a WADL file to demonstrate how it is used by other clients for discovery.

The following listing shows a sample WADL file describing the resources available at `/catalog`, `/catalog/v2/{categoryId}`:

```xml
<?xml version="1.0" encoding="UTF-8"?>
<application xmlns="http://wadl.dev.java.net/2009/02"
xmlns:service="http://localhost:8080/catalog/"
xmlns:xsd="http://www.w3.org/2001/XMLSchema">
   <grammer>
      <include href="items.xsd" />
      <include href="error.xsd" />
   </grammer>
   <resources base="http://localhost:8080/catalog/">
      <resource path="{categoryId}">
```

```
            <method name="GET">
                <request>
                    <param name="category" type="xsd:string" style="template" />
                </request>
                <response status="200">
                    <representation mediaType="application/xml"
element="service:item" />
                    <representation mediaType="application/json" />
                </response>
                <response status="404">
                    <representation mediaType="text/plain"
element="service:item" />
                </response>
            </method>
        </resource>
        <resource path="/v2/{categoryId}">
            <method name="GET">
                <request>
                    <param name="category" type="xsd:string" style="template" />
                </request>
                <response status="200">
                    <representation mediaType="application/xml"
element="service:item" />
                    <representation mediaType="application/json" />
                </response>
                <response status="404">
                    <representation mediaType="text/plain"
element="service:item" />
                </response>
            </method>
        </resource>
    </resources>
</application>
```

As you can see, the WADL format is very straightforward. It basically describes the URI of each resource, providing information about the media types it uses and the status codes that are expected at that URI. Many third-party RESTful clients understand the WADL language and can generate request messages out of a given WADL file.

Let's import the WADL file in Postman. Click on the **Import** button and select your WADL file:

Import a WADL in Postman to get a stub of the service. This is a screenshot for Postman. The individual settings are not important here. The purpose of the image is just to show how the window looks.

As you can see, the result of importing the WADL file is that we have a project ready to test each aspect of a REST service in the nick of time. All the routes defined in the WADL file are now conveniently available as separate request entities on the right menu. That's not all; apart from the WADL standard, currently the swagger documentation format is heavily adopted and has become an informal standard for describing RESTful services, so we can also use it to ease the adoption and discovery of our service. In the next chapter, we will bind these description files to our service. This is an important step in the phase of production preparation.

Summary

Congratulations! In this chapter, you succeeded in transforming a sample REST-enabled endpoint into a full-fledged RESTful web service that supports filtering for usability and paging for easy navigation. The service delivers both arbitrary and JSON data, and it is ready for high-load scenarios, as it enables caching in its critical parts. One thing that should draw your attention is the appropriate usage of the HTTP status codes when it comes to redirection between new and obsolete versions of any public API.

Implementing appropriate HTTP status is really important for the REST application, so we made use of rather exotic statuses, such as 301 Moved Permanently and 302 Found. In the next chapter, we will introduce the concept of authorization into our application.

7
Preparing a RESTful API for Production

In the previous chapter, we implemented a full fledged catalog RESTful API; however, there is a difference between a completely functional API and a production-ready one. In this chapter, we will cover how an API should be documented and tested thoroughly. These key requirements have to be completed by any piece of software before going productive.

To sum up, in this chapter, we will cover the following topics:

- Documenting RESTful APIs
- Testing RESTful APIs with Mocha
- The microservices revolution

Documenting RESTful APIs

Until now, we partially covered how RESTful web services APIs are described by wadl and documented by swagger specifications. Now it's time to take full advantage of them and expose their self-descriptive metadata in express.js routes in our catalog application. That way, both consumers and end users will have separate URLs for the metadata they will need to adopt the service easily. Let's start with the wadl definitions. Here's how an operation is fully described by wadl:

```
<resources base="http://localhost:8080/catalog/">
    <resource path="/catalog/item/{itemId}">
        <method name="GET">
            <request>
                <param name="category" type="xsd:string"
style="template"/>
            </request>
            <response status="200">
                <representation mediaType="application/json" />
            </response>
            <response status="404">
                <representation mediaType="text/plain" />
            </response>
            <response status="500">
                <representation mediaType="text/plain" />
            </response>
        </method>
        <method name="PUT">
            <request>
                <param name="itemId" type="xsd:string"
style="template"/>
            </request>
            <response status="200">
                <representation mediaType="application/json" />
            </response>
            <response status="201">
                <representation mediaType="application/json" />
            </response>
            <response status="404">
                <representation mediaType="text/plain" />
            </response>
            <response status="500">
                <representation mediaType="text/plain" />
            </response>
        </method>
        <method name="POST">
            <request>
```

```xml
                <param name="itemId" type="xsd:string"
                 style="template"/>
            </request>
            <response status="200">
                <representation mediaType="application/json" />
            </response>
            <response status="201">
                <representation mediaType="application/json" />
            </response>
            <response status="404">
                <representation mediaType="text/plain" />
            </response>
            <response status="500">
                <representation mediaType="text/plain" />
            </response>
        </method>
        <method name="DELETE">
            <request>
                <param name="itemId" type="xsd:string"
                 style="template"/>
            </request>
            <response status="200">
                <representation mediaType="application/json" />
            </response>
            <response status="404">
                <representation mediaType="text/plain" />
            </response>
            <response status="500">
                <representation mediaType="text/plain" />
            </response>
        </method>
    </resource>
    </resources>
```

Each route thoroughly describes all the operations it exposes; that way, they will be indexed and discoverable by clients compliant with the `wadl` specification. Once you have all your operations described, simply store the `wadl` file in the `static` directory of your `express.js` project and expose it from application: `app.use('/catalog/static', express.static('static'));`

After starting your application locally, your `wadl` file will be ready to serve clients at `http://localhost:3000/catalog/static/catalog.wadl`.

Let's give that a try and import it to Postman:

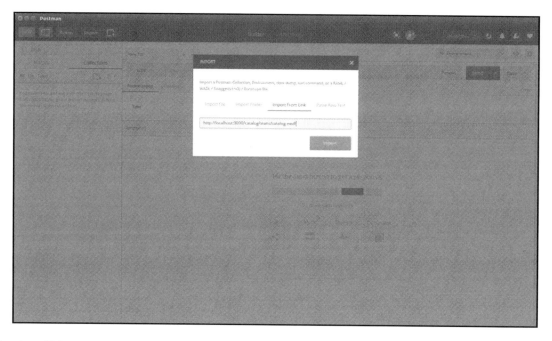

Importing wadl file into Postman. This is a screenshot for Postman. The individual settings are not important here. The purpose of the image is just to show how the window looks.

Serving the `wadl` file statically will help your application in getting indexed by search engines; this further increases the adoption of your API.

However, slowly but surely, `wadl` is losing grip in favor of `swagger`. The evolution of JavaScript REST-enabled applications has led to the requirement of the non-XML based standard for discovering RESTful services. That is the reason for `swagger` to become the de facto standard, not only for documenting RESTful services, but also for its widely adopted discovery format. While XML-aware platforms are still relying on `wadl`, JavaScript and other non XML-native platforms are heavily relying on the `swagger` specification, not only for description but also for discovery and consumption, and its adoption is progressing rapidly. So you should consider having your APIs described in `swagger` to ensure easy adoption from any platform out there. Here's how an operation is fully described in a `swagger` dialect:

```
{
    "swagger": "2.0",
    "info": {
        "title": "Catalog API Documentation",
```

```
      "version": "v1"
    },
    "paths": {"/catalog/item/{itemId}": {
        "get": {
          "operationId": "getItemV2",
          "summary": "Get an existing item",
          "produces": ["application/json"],
          "responses": {
            "200": {
              "description": "200 OK",
              "examples": {
                "application/json": {
                    "_id": "5a4c004b0eed73835833cc9a",
                    "itemId": "1",
                    "itemName": "Sports Watch",
                    "price": 100,
                    "currency": "EUR",
                    "__v": 0,
                    "categories": [ "Watches", "Sports Watches"]
                  }
                }
            },
            "404": {"description": "404 Not Found"},
            "500": {"description": "500 Internal Server Error"}
          }
        },
        "post": {
          "404": {"description": "404 Not Found"},
          "500": {"description": "500 Internal Server Error"},
          "operationId": "postItemV2",
          "summary": "Creates new or updates existing item",
          "produces": ["application/json"],
          "responses": {
            "200": {
              "itemId": 19,
              "itemName": "Sports Watch 19",
              "price": 100,
              "currency": "USD",
              "__v": 0,
              "categories": [
                "Watches",
                "Sports Watches"
              ]
            },
            "201": {
              "itemId": 19,
              "itemName": "Sports Watch 19",
              "price": 100,
```

```
            "currency": "USD",
            "__v": 0,
            "categories": [ "Watches", "Sports Watches"]
          },
          "500": "text/html"
        }
      },
      "put": {
        "404": {"description": "404 Not Found"},
        "500": {"description": "500 Internal Server Error"},
        "operationId": "putItemV2",
        "summary": "Creates new or updates existing item",
        "produces": ["application/json"],
        "responses": {
          "200": {
            "itemId": 19,
            "itemName": "Sports Watch 19",
            "price": 100,
            "currency": "USD",
            "__v": 0,
            "categories": [ "Watches","Sports Watches"]
          },
          "201": {
            "itemId": 19,
            "itemName": "Sports Watch 19",
            "price": 100,
            "currency": "USD",
            "__v": 0,
            "categories": ["Watches", "Sports Watches"]
          },
          "500": "text/html"
        }
      },
      "delete": {
        "404": {"description": "404 Not Found"},
        "500": {"description": "500 Internal Server Error"},
        "operationId": "deleteItemV2",
        "summary": "Deletes an existing item",
        "produces": ["application/json"],
        "responses": {"200": {"deleted": true },
          "500": "text/html"}
      }
    }
  }
  consumes": ["application/json"]
  }
}
```

Finally, after having all the APIs' operations described in a `swagger.json` file, it should be statically exposed, similar to the `wadl` file. Since the application already has a route for the static directory, just place the `swagger.json` file there, and it will be ready for serving consumers and promoting discovery. `Swagger`, being mainly a documentation tool, however, mainly targets developers; thus, it needs a frontend that makes the documentation easy to read and understand. There is an `npm` module—`swagger-ui`—that wraps up the default swagger frontend for us. We will adopt it in our application, so let's use the package manager to install it—`npm install swagger-ui`. Once installed, simply require an instance of the module along with an instance of the static `swagger.json` file and use them in a separate route:

```
const swaggerUi = require('swagger-ui-express');
const swaggerDocument = require('./static/swagger.json');

app.use('/catalog/api-docs', swaggerUi.serve,
swaggerUi.setup(swaggerDocument));
```

Start your application and request `http://localhost:3000/catalog/api-docs/` in a browser:

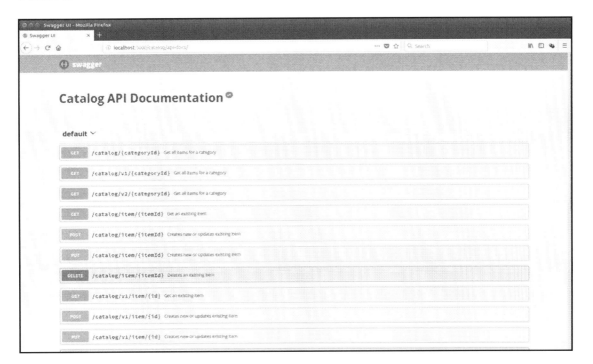

As you can see, the swagger-ui module provided the standard swagger frontend for you.

 Keep in mind that, as a developer, keeping your API documentation in a shape and up to date is your responsibility.

Testing RESTful APIs with Mocha

Have you noted that the app.js express application created with express-generator is actually a node.js module exporting the express instance? In case you have, you must have asked yourself why that is actually needed. Well, having the express instance exported as a module enables it to be unit-tested. We already utilized the mocha framework in Chapter 4, *Using NoSQL Databases*, where we developed a unit test for the CatalogItem module. We will use mocha once again and wrap a unit test around each operation API exposes. To unit-test the express application, we will need to do the following:

1. Require an instance to the express.js application with the routes, making use of its being exported as a module
2. Start the express.js instance in unit test environment
3. Invoke its operations via a test library and assert against the results
4. Finally, execute the npm test command to trigger the unit test

Before moving on and implementing mocha tests, we need a library for sending HTTP requests from the unit tests; we will make use of the chai module. It provides convenient functions for sending HTTP requests, and it also bundles the should.js assertion library to verify the expected results. To install chai, simply execute npm install chai and then its npm install chai-http HTTP plugin, and we are ready to start unit testing!

As with any other mocha test, we will have to carry out the given steps:

1. Describe each test case
2. Prepare the test fixture; this time, we will be using chai-http for invoking the rest operations
3. Assert against the returned results

A basic unit test covering the operations for creating, accessing, and deleting resources looks like the following:

```
var expressApp = require('../../app');
```

```
var chai = require('chai');
var chaiHttp = require('chai-http');
var mongoose = require('mongoose');
var should = chai.should();

mongoose.createConnection('mongodb://localhost/catalog-test');

chai.use(chaiHttp);

describe('/get', function() {
  it('get test', function(done) {
    chai.request(expressApp)
      .get('/catalog/v2')
      .end(function(error, response) {
        should.equal(200   , response.status);
        done();
      });
    });
  });

describe('/post', function() {
    it('post test', function(done) {
      var item ={
         "itemId":19,
         "itemName": "Sports Watch 10",
         "price": 100,
         "currency": "USD",
         "__v": 0,
         "categories": [
             "Watches",
             "Sports Watches"
         ]
      };
    chai.request(expressApp)
         .post('/catalog/v2')
         .send(item )
         .end(function(err, response){
             should.equal(201, response.status)
           done();
         });
    });
  });

  describe('/delete', function() {
      it('delete test', function(done) {
         var item ={
            "itemId":19,
            "itemName": "Sports Watch 10",
```

```
            "price": 100,
            "currency": "USD",
            "__v"cd .: 0,
            "categories": [
                "Watches",
                "Sports Watches"
            ]
        };
    chai.request(expressApp)
            .delete('/catalog/v2/item/19')
            .send(item )
            .end(function(err, response){
                should.equal(200, response.status)
              done();
            });
        });
    });
```

Store this file in the test directory of your project; this directory is defined as a test directory in the package.json by default, so to run the unit test, just execute npm test:

Congratulations! Now you have your API covered with unit tests, and note that the tests aren't mocking anything! They are running the express application; exactly the same way, the application will be run when it becomes productive, ensuring stability and backward compatibility! Currently, the unit test asserts only against status code. Spend some time with it and extend them further to assert against the response body as well. This will be a good exercise.

The microservices revolution

It wasn't very long ago when the RESTful API madness started and almost everyone decided that RESTful APIs were the right way to go, was it? With `Linux` containers available, it turned out that switching to the REST approach was only half of the way. Currently, everyone is benefiting from containers. They provide better, faster, and cheaper development and operational model, but are microservices just yet another buzz term for RESTful services? Well, no, not at all; RESTful services are just the foundation of microservices.

Microservices are small and independent processes exposing a simple interface that allows communication with them and building complex applications without depending on library artefacts. These services resemble small building blocks, highly decoupled and focused on doing a small task, facilitating a modular approach to system-building.

While REST emphasizes on resources and their natural handling, the microservices architecture emphasizes on simplicity, fail-safeness, and isolation. A RESTful API doesn't have separate states per operation; it is either that the entire API is available or it is completely down. Microservices attempt to solve that problem, providing means to host each operation on a separate container, or subset of containers, ensuring maximum fault tolerance and agility.

A microservice is expected to provide a single simple action, nothing more. This enables developers to group and consume them exactly the way they want. Policy handling, governance, security, and monitoring are usually out of the scope when dealing with microservices, mainly because they require some kind of context. In general, binding context to a service increases its dependencies and makes it less reusable; this is why microservices leave context to API management gateways, which allow you to create a composite of microservices and then bind a policy to it and monitor every activity on the gateway. This distribution development model empowers programmers to rapidly grow a collection of microservices without considering complex topics such as governance and security.

The microservices world is a game changer, benefiting from Linux containers. Currently, all cloud-based offerings similar to AWS and Azure provide microservices hosting.

Summary

In this chapter, we stepped slightly aside from `Express.js` related topics. Instead, we concentrated on how to productionize our code base by providing up-to-date API documentation, along with the API itself. We had our application invest in precautionary measures for ensuring backward compatibility by implementing more complex unit tests that actually target close-to-real-life implementation. Finally, we decided to look into the future, which is all about microservices. Ensure that you keep this hot topic up in your skill-list; it will inevitably evolve in the near future, and the more you know about it, the better!

Consuming a RESTful API

8

To demonstrate some more advanced topics related to the consumption of our API, we will implement a really simple web client. It will help us cover those topics, and it can serve as a reference implementation for the catalog's consumers. For this frontend client, we will use the famous JavaScript library, jQuery. Utilizing it will help us cover the following:

- Consuming RESTful services with jQuery
- Content Delivery Network
- Troubleshooting and identifying problems on the wire
- Cross-Origin Resource Sharing policy
- Client-side handling of different HTTP status codes

Consuming RESTful services with jQuery

JQuery is a fast, light, and powerful JavaScript library; it eliminates DOM-related complexity by providing direct access to HTML elements once the DOM three has been loaded. To use jQuery within an HTML document, you have to import it:

```
<script type="text/javascript"
src="https://code.jquery.com/jquery-3.3.1.min.js "></script>
```

Assume that somewhere within an HTML document, there is a button defined as `<input type="button" id="btnDelete" value="Delete"/>`.

To assign a function to the click event of this button with JQuery means we need to do the following:

1. Import the jquery library in the HTML document
2. Assure that the DOM document of the HTML document is completely loaded
3. Access the button using the identifier defined by the ID attribute
4. Provide a handler function as an argument to the click event:

```
$(document).ready(function() {
    $('#btn').click(function () {
        alert('Clicked');
    });
});
```

The $('#identifier') expression provides direct access to elements in DOM three, $ states that an object is referenced, and the value within the bracket, prefix by # specifies its identifier. jQuery will have access to the element only after the entire document has been loaded; that's why elements should be accessed within ${document}.ready() block scope.

Similarly, you can access the value of a text input with an identifier txt:

```
$(document).ready(function() {
    var textValue = $('#txt').val();
    });
});
```

The $(document) object is predefined in jQuery and represents the entire DOM document of the HTML page. In a similar way, jQuery predefines a function for AJAX-enabled communication, that is, for sending HTTP request to an HTTP endpoint. This function is named after **Asynchronous JavaScript + XML-** AJAX, which was the de facto standard that enabled a JavaScript application to communicate with HTTP-enabled backends. Nowadays, **JSON** is being widely used; however, naming conversion for AJAX is still used as a term for asynchronous communication, regardless of the data format; that is why the predefined function in jQuery is called $.ajax(options, handlers).

To send an http request with the $.ajax function, invoke it by providing the endpoint URL, http method for the request, and its content type; the result will be returned in a callback function. The following example shows how an item with identifier 3 is requested from our catalog:

```
$.ajax({
    contentType: 'application/json',
    url: 'http://localhost:3000/catalog/v2/item/3',
    type: 'GET',
    success: function (item, status, xhr) {
        if (status === 'success') {
            //the item is successfully retrieved load & display its
details here
        }
    }
    ,error: function (xhr, options, error) {
      //Item was not retrieved due to an error handle it here
    }
  });
});
```

Posting data to an endpoint is rather similar:

```
$.ajax({
  url: "http://localhost:3000/catalog/v2/",
  type: "POST",
  dataType: "json",
  data: JSON.stringify(newItem),
   success: function (item, status, xhr) {
     if (status === 'success') {
       //item was created successfully
     }
   },
   error: function(xhr, options, error) {
     //Error occurred while creating the iteam
   }
  });
```

Simply use the appropriate options type set to POST, and the dateType set to JSON. Those will specify that a POST request is to be sent to the endpoint in the JSON format. The payload of the object is provided as a value to the data attribute.

Invoking a `delete` method is quite similar:

```
$.ajax({
    contentType: 'application/json',
    url: 'http://localhost:3000/catalog/v2/item/3',
    type: 'DELETE',
    success: function (item, status, xhr) {
        if (status === 'success') {
            //handle successful deletion
        }
    }
    ,error: function (xhr, options, error) {
        //handle errors on delete
    }
});
```

A basic understanding of how jQuery works is just about fine for the scope of this book. Now, let's glue all this together and create two HTML pages; that way, we will handle creating, displaying, and deleting an item in our catalog, starting with the page that displays an item and allows its deletion. This page loads an item from the catalog using GET request, and then displays the item's attributes in the HTML page in a table-like manner:

```
<html>
<head><title>Item</title></head>
<body>
    <script type="text/javascript"
src="https://code.jquery.com/jquery-3.3.1.min.js "></script>
  <script>
  $(document).ready(function() {
    $('#btnDelete').click(function () {
      $.ajax({
        contentType: 'application/json',
        url: 'http://localhost:3000/catalog/v2/item/3',
        type: 'DELETE',
        success: function (item, status, xhr) {
            if (status === 'success') {
               $('#item').text('Deleted');
               $('#price').text('Deleted');
               $('#categories').text('Deleted');
            }
        }
        ,error: function (xhr, options, error) {
          alert('Unable to delete item');
        }
      });
    });
    $.ajax({
```

```
        contentType: 'application/json',
        url: 'http://localhost:3000/catalog/v2/item/3',
        type: 'GET',
        success: function (item, status, xhr) {
            if (status === 'success') {
              $('#item').text(item.itemName);
              $('#price').text(item.price + ' ' + item.currency);
              $('#categories').text(item.categories);
            }
        }
        ,error: function (xhr, options, error) {
          alert('Unable to load details');
        }
      });
    });
  </script>
  <div>
    <div style="position: relative">
      <div style="float:left; width: 80px;">Item: </div>
      <div><span id="item"/>k</div>
    </div>
    <div style="position: relative">
      <div style="float:left; width: 80px;">Price: </div>
      <div><span id="price"/>jjj</div>
    </div>
    <div style="position: relative">
      <div style="float:left; width: 80px;">Categories: </div>
      <div><span id="categories"/>jjj</div>
    </div>
    <div><input type="button" id="btnDelete" value="Delete"/></div>
  </div>
</body>
</html>
```

The page that handles creation is quite similar. However, it provides text inputs instead of span labels for an item's fields, where the view page will display the data for the attributes of the loaded item. JQuery provides a simplified access model to the input controls, rather than DOM—simply access the input element as follows:

```
<html>
<head><title>Item</title></head>
<body>
  <script type="text/javascript"
src="https://code.jquery.com/jquery-3.3.1.min.js "></script>
  <script>
  $(document).ready(function() {
    $('#btnCreate').click(function(){
```

```
      var txtItemName = $('#txtItem').val();
      var txtItemPrice = $('#txtItemPrice').val();
      var txtItemCurrency = $('#txtItemCurrency').val();
      var newItem = {
        itemId: 4,
        itemName: txtItemName,
        price: txtItemPrice,
        currency: txtItemCurrency,
        categories: [
          "Watches"
        ]
      };
      $.ajax({
        url: "http://localhost:3000/catalog/v2/",
        type: "POST",
        dataType: "json",
        data: JSON.stringify(newItem),
        success: function (item, status, xhr) {
            alert(status);
          }
      });
    })
  });
  </script>
  <div>
    <div style="position: relative">
      <div style="float:left; width: 80px;">Id: </div>
      <div><input type="text" id="id"/></div>

      <div style="float:left; width: 80px;">Item: </div>
      <div><input type="text" id="txtItem"/></div>
    </div>
    <div style="position: relative">
      <div style="float:left; width: 80px;">Price: </div>
      <div><input type="text" id="price"/></div>
    </div>
    <div style="position: relative">
      <div style="float:left; width: 80px;">Categories: </div>
      <div><input type="text" id="categories"/></div>
    </div>
    <div><input type="button" id="btnCreate" value="Create"/></div>
  </div>
</body>
</html>
```

Let's give that a try and load an existing item in the view page by opening our static page directly from the filesystem in a browser of your choice. It looks as if we have some kind of a problem, as nothing gets displayed. Enabling client-side debugging using the browser's developer suite doesn't give much more information either:

It states that the content is partially blocked; however, it is not quite clear whether this is due to a backend-related error, or something has gone wrong on the client side. We will look at how to troubleshoot such problematic situations in the next section.

Troubleshooting and identifying problems on the wire

Sometimes the interaction between the client and the server fails, and the reason for such failures often requires analysis; otherwise, their root cause stays unknown. We spotted that our client application does not load and thus doesn't display data for an existing item. Let's try to investigate the root cause for that by setting up an `http` tunnel between the client and the server. This will be a kind of MiM (man-in-the-middle)-based investigation, as we will listen to one port and redirect the incoming request to another, to see whether the server returns correct responses or its pipe gets broken somewhere in the middle. There are various TCP tunnels available out there; I have been using a simple open source one available on GitHub at `https://github.com/vakuum/tcptunnel`. Its author also maintains a separate website where you can download prebuilt binaries for the most common operating system; they are available at `http://www.vakuumverpackt.de/tcptunnel/`.

After you have built or downloaded a copy of the tunnel, start it as follows:

```
./tcptunnel --local-port=3001 --remote-port=3000 --remote-
host=localhost --log
```

This will start the application listening on port 3001 and will forward each incoming request to location port 3000; the `--log` option specifies that all the data flow passing the tunnel should be logged in the console. Finally, modify HTML pages to use port 3001 instead of 3000, and let's see what the tunnel would show us after firing new GET request for the item with id 3, this time on port 3001: `http://localhost:3001/catalog/v2/item/3`:

```
valio@G771JW: ~/git/tcptunnel
valio@G771JW:~/git/tcptunnel$ ./tcptunnel --local-port=3001 --remote-port=3000 --remote-host=localhost --log
> 2018-03-26 01:57:40 tcptunnel: request from 127.0.0.1
> 2018-03-26 01:57:40 > GET /catalog/v2/item/3 HTTP/1.1
Host: localhost:3001
Connection: keep-alive
Cache-Control: no-cache
Content-Type: application/json
User-Agent: Mozilla/5.0 (X11; Linux x86_64) AppleWebKit/537.36 (KHTML, like Gecko) Chrome/67.0.3377.1 Safari/537.36
Postman-Token: 917e1dfd-b00b-fb5b-3019-1e47bda13708
Accept: */*
Accept-Encoding: gzip, deflate, br
Accept-Language: en-US,en;q=0.9

HTTP/1.1 200 OK
X-Powered-By: Express
Content-Type: application/json; charset=utf-8
Image-Url: http://localhost:3001/catalog/v2/item/3/image
Content-Length: 137
ETag: W/"89-onqoMr/67e303rbPFZKMhCIQ+fU"
Date: Sun, 25 Mar 2018 22:57:40 GMT
Connection: keep-alive

{"_id":"5ab827f65d61450e40d7d984","itemId":"3","itemName":"Sports Watch 11","price":99,"currency":"USD","__v":0,"categor
ies":["Watches"]}valio@G771JW:~/git/tcptunnel$ 
```

Surprisingly, the tunnel shows that the server responds normally with `200 OK` and a relevant payload. So it seems as if the problem is not on the server side.

Well, since the error is obviously not on the server side, let's try to investigate deeper what has happened on the client side. Nowadays, all popular browsers have so-called web developer tools. They provide access to `http` logs, dynamically-rendered code, the DOM three of the HTML document, and so on. Let's invoke our RESTful GET operation with Mozillas Firefox and see what its web console will log about our request. Open the Mozilla Firefox menu and select `Web Developer`, and then select `Browser Console`:

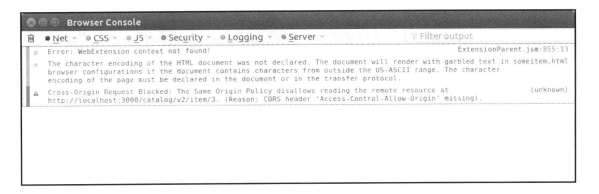

Aha! Seems like we found it: `Cross-Origin Request Blocked: The Same Origin Policy disallows reading the remove resource at....`

This error is blocking the server-side response at client level. In the next section, we will see what this actually means.

Cross Origin Resource Sharing

Cross-site HTTP requests are requests that refer to resources to be loaded from a domain different from the one that initially requested them. In our case, we started the client from our filesystem, and it requested resources from a network address. This is considered a potential **Cross-site scripting** request, which, according to the **W3C recommendation** at `http://w3.org/cors/TR/cors`, should be carefully handled. This means that if an external resource is requested, the domain where it is requested from—its Origin—should be explicitly specified in a header, as long as an external resource loading is not allowed in general. This mechanism prevents Cross-Side Scripting (XSS) attacks, and it is based on HTTP headers.

The following HTTP request headers specify how external resources should be handled on the client side:

- `Origin` defines where the request originated from
- `Access-Control-Request-Method` defines the HTTP method that was used to request the resource
- `Access-Control-Request-Header` defines any headers that will be allowed in combination with the external resource request

On the server side, the following headers indicate whether a response is eligible for a CORS-enabled client request:

- `Access-Control-Allow-Origin`: This header either, if exists, specifies that the requester's host is allowed by repeating it, or it could specify that all remote origins are allowed by returning a wildcard: '*'
- `Access-Control-Allow-Methods`: This header specifies the HTTP methods that the server would allow from cross-side's domain
- `Access-Control-Allow-Headers`: This header specifies the HTTP headers that the server would allow from cross-side's domain

There are some more `Access-Control-*` headers that can be used for further granularity when incoming XSS requests are to be served, or not, based on credentials and request's max-age, but basically, the most important ones are for the allowed origin, allowed methods, and allowed headers.

There is a node module that handles CORS configuration at server side; it is installed by `npm install -g cors` and is easily enabled in our application via a middleware module. Simply use it in all the exposed routes by passing it to the application:

```
app.use(cors());
```

Use the tunnel after you enabled the `cors` middleware to see that the server would now gracefully handle requests from different origins by serving the "Access-Control-Allow-Origin' header set to '*'":

```
valio@G771JW: ~/git/tcptunnel
valio@G771JW:~/git/tcptunnel$
valio@G771JW:~/git/tcptunnel$ ./tcptunnel --local-port=3001 --remote-port=3000 --remote-host=localhost --log
> 2018-03-26 01:51:54 tcptunnel: request from 127.0.0.1
> 2018-03-26 01:51:54 > GET /catalog/v2/item/3 HTTP/1.1
Host: localhost:3001
Connection: keep-alive
Cache-Control: no-cache
Content-Type: application/json
User-Agent: Mozilla/5.0 (X11; Linux x86_64) AppleWebKit/537.36 (KHTML, like Gecko) Chrome/67.0.3377.1 Safari/537.36
Postman-Token: 100ae78b-b8f8-353f-f5f8-6c0b5e9a9ec2
Accept: */*
Accept-Encoding: gzip, deflate, br
Accept-Language: en-US,en;q=0.9

HTTP/1.1 200 OK
X-Powered-By: Express
Access-Control-Allow-Origin: *
Content-Type: application/json; charset=utf-8
Image-Url: http://localhost:3001/catalog/v2/item/3/image
Content-Length: 137
ETag: W/"89-onqoMr/67e303rbPFZKMhCIQ+fU"
Date: Sun, 25 Mar 2018 22:51:54 GMT
Connection: keep-alive

{"_id":"5ab827f65d61450e40d7d984","itemId":"3","itemName":"Sports Watch 11","price":99,"currency":"USD","__v":0,"categor
ies":["Watches"]}valio@G771JW:~/git/tcptunnel$
```

Content Delivery Networks

When we imported the jQuery library into our client application, we directly referred to its optimized source from its vendor as `<script type="text/javascript" src="https://code.jquery.com/jquery-3.3.1.min.js "/>`.

Now, imagine that for some reason this site goes down either temporarily or for good; this will make our application unusable, as the import wouldn't work.

Content Delivery Networks come to help in these cases. They serve as a repository for libraries or other static media content, assuring that the needed resources will be available without downtime, even when something goes wrong with their vendors. One of the most popular JavaScript CDNs is `https://cdnjs.com/`; it provides the most common JS libraries available out there. We will switch our clients to refer to the jquery library from this CDN rather than from its vendors' website at `<script type="text/javascript" src="https://code.jquery.com/jquery-3.3.1.min.js "/>`.

While there is hardly anything wrong with directly downloading your JS libraries and placing them in the static directory of your node.js project, it may lead to having local changes and fixes directly in your library dependencies. This can easily result in incompatible changes and can prevent your application from easily switching to newer versions in the future. As long as your dependencies are open source, you should strive to improve them by contributing fixes or reporting bugs rather than having fixes in your own local fork. Still, if you are unfortunate enough to run into a bug that you can easily fix, you can fork the library to resolve your problem faster. However, always consider contributing the fix back to the community. After it is accepted, switch back to the official version; otherwise, you will find yourself in a difficult situation the next time with another issue, and the community would track it much harder if reported from a forked version. That is the beauty of open source, and that is why you should always consider consuming JavaScript APIs' Content Delivery Networks. They will provide you with the stability and support you may need at any point in the life of your application.

Handling HTTP status codes on the client side

We spent quite some time addressing how RESTful services should represent each state, including erroneous ones, gracefully. A well-defined API should demand from its consumers to handle all its errors gracefully and to provide as much information per state as required, rather than just stating "An error has occurred". That is why it should look up the returned status code and clearly distinguish between client requests such as 400 Bad Request or 415 Unsupported media types caused by faulty payload, caused by wrong media types, or authentication-related errors, such as 401 Unauthorized.

The status code of an erroneous response is available in the error callback of the jQuery callback function and should be used to provide detailed information back to the request:

```
$.ajax({
    url: "http://localhost:3000/catalog/v2/",
    type: "POST",
    dataType: "json",
    data: JSON.stringify(newItem),
    success: function (item, status, jqXHR) {
        alert(status);
    },
    error: function(jqXHR, statusText, error) {
        switch(jqXHR.status) {
            case 400: alert('Bad request'); break;
            case 401: alert('Unauthroizaed'); break;
            case 404: alert('Not found'); break;
            //handle any other client errors below
            case 500: alert('Internal server error); break;
            //handle any other server errors below
        }
    }
});
```

Unsuccessful requests are handled by the error callback function. It provides jqXHR - the XmlHttpRequest JavaScript—object as its first argument. It carries across all the request/response related information, such as status code and headers. Use it to determine what the requested server has returned so that your application can handle different errors more granularly.

Summary

In this chapter, we implemented a simple web-based client with the jQuery library. We utilized this client to demonstrate how the Cross-Origin Resource Sharing policy works, and we used a man in the middle means to troubleshoot issues on the wire. Finally, we looked at how errors should be handled on the client side. This chapter brings us one step closer to the end of our journey, as we got the first consumer of our service. In the next chapter, we will walk you through the final step before bringing a service to production—choosing its security model.

Securing the Application

9

Once deployed in production, an application is exposed to a large number of requests. Inevitably, some of them will be malicious. This brings the requirement of granting explicit access permissions only to authenticated users, that is, authenticating a selected number of consumers to have access to your service. Most of the consumers will use the service only for data provisioning. However, a few will need to be able to provide new, or modify the existing, catalog data. To ensure that only appropriate consumers will be able to execute the POST, PUT, and DELETE requests, we will have to introduce the concept of authorization into our application, which will grant only explicitly selected users modification permissions.

Data services may provide sensitive private information, such as email addresses; the HTTP protocol, being a text protocol, may not be secure enough. The information transmitted through it is subject to **man-in-the-middle** attacks, which can lead to data leakage. To prevent such cases, **Transport Layer Security** (**TLS**) should be used. The HTTPS protocol encrypts the transmitted data, ensuring that only appropriate consumers who have the right decryption key will be able to consume the data exposed by the service.

In this chapter, we will look at how Node.js enables the following security features:

- Basic authentication
- Passport-based basic authentication
- Passport-based third-party authentication
- Authorization
- Transport layer security

Authentication

An application considers a user authenticated when their identity has been successfully validated against a trusted store. Such trusted stores can either be any kind of specially maintained database, storing the credentials of the application (basic authentication), or a third-party service that checks a given identity against its own trusted store (third-party authentication).

Basic authentication

HTTP basic authentication is one of the most popular and straightforward authentication mechanisms available out there. It relies on HTTP headers in the request, which provide the user's credentials. Optionally, the server may reply with a header, forcing the clients to authenticate themselves. The following diagram shows a client-server interaction when basic authentication is carried out:

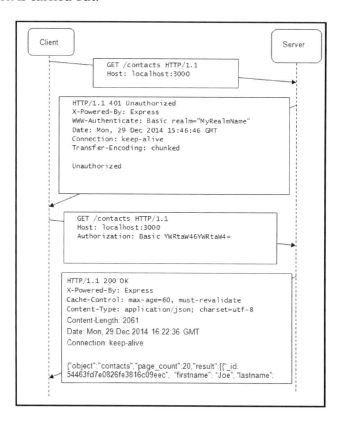

Whenever an HTTP request is sent to an endpoint secured by HTTP basic authentication, the server replies with an HTTP `401 Unauthorized` status code, and, optionally, with a `WWW-Authenticate` header. This header forces the client to send another request, containing the `Authorization` header, which specifies that the authentication method is `basic`. This request is followed by a base64-encoded key/value pair, providing the username and the password to authenticate with. Optionally, the server can specify a message to the client with the `realm` attribute.

This attribute specifies that resources sharing the same `realm` value should support the same authentication means. In the preceding diagram, the `realm` message is `MyRealmName`. The client authenticates by sending the `Authentication` header with the value of `Basic YWRtaW46YWRtaW4`, specifying that `Basic` authentication is used, followed by the base64-encoded value. In the diagram, the literal `YWRtaW46YWRtaW4` decoded in base64 represents the `admin:admin` literal. In case such a username/password combination is successfully authenticated, the HTTP server will respond with the JSON payload of the requested items. If the authentication fails, the server will respond with the `401 Unauthorized` status code, but this time without including the `WWW-Authenticate` header.

Passport

There are plenty of authentication methods to choose from nowadays. Perhaps the most popular methods are basic authentication, where each user has their own username and password, and third-party authentication, where users can identify themselves with their already-existing account for an external public service, such as personal social services such as LinkedIn, Facebook, and Twitter.

Choosing the most appropriate type of authentication for a web API depends mainly on its consumers. Apparently, an application consuming an API to fetch data is not likely to authenticate with a personal social account. This approach is more suitable when the API is used via a frontend directly by a human being.

Implementing a solution capable of switching between different authentication methods easily is a complex and time-consuming task. In fact, it can become hardly possible if not considered at the initial design phase of an application.

Passport is a piece of authentication middleware for Node.js, created especially for use-cases where the means of authentication should be easily switched from one to another. It has modular architecture that enables the usage of a specific authentication provider, called **strategy**. The strategy takes care of implementing a chosen authentication approach.

There are plenty of authentication strategies to choose from, for example, a regular basic authentication strategy or social platform-based strategies for services such as Facebook, LinkedIn, and Twitter. Refer to the official Passport website, `http://www.passportjs.org/`, for a complete list of the available strategies.

Passport's basic authentication strategy

Now it is time to look at how to utilize Passport's strategies; we will start with the basic authentication strategy; it is a logical choice now that we know how basic authentication works.

As usual, we will start by installing the relevant modules with the NPM package manager. We will need the `passport` module, which provides the base functionality that allows you to plug in different authentication strategies, and a concrete strategy for basic authentication, provided by the `passport-http` module:

```
npm install passport
npm install passport-http
```

Next, we have to instantiate both the Passport middleware and the basic authentication strategy. `BasicStrategy` takes as an argument a callback function, which checks whether the provided username/password combination is valid. Finally, passport's authenticate method is provided as a middleware function to the express route, assuring that unauthenticated requests will be rejected with an appropriate `401 Unauthorized` status:

```
const passport = require('passport');
const BasicStrategy = require('passport-http').BasicStrategy;

passport.use(new BasicStrategy(function(username, password, done) {
  if (username == 'user' && password=='default') {
    return done(null, username);
  }
}));

router.get('/v1/',
  passport.authenticate('basic', { session: false }),
    function(request,    response, next) {
      catalogV1.findAllItems(response);
});
router.get('/v2/',
  passport.authenticate('basic', { session: false }),
    function(request,    response, next) {
      catalogV1.findAllItems(response);
});
```

```
router.get('/',
  passport.authenticate('basic', { session: false }),
    function(request,     response, next) {
      catalogV1.findAllItems(response);
});
```

The `BasicStrategy` constructor takes a handler function as an argument. It gives us access to the username and password supplied by the client, and to the Passport middleware's `done()` function, which notifies Passport with whether the user has been successfully authenticated. Invoke the `done()` function with `user` as an argument in order to grant authentication, or pass the `error` argument to it to revoke the authentication:

```
passport.use(new BasicStrategy(
function(username, password, done) {
  AuthUser.findOne({username: username, password: password},
    function(error, user) {
      if (error) {
        return done(error);
      } else {
        if (!user) {
          console.log('unknown user');
          return done(error);
        } else {
          console.log(user.username + '
          authenticated successfully');
          return done(null, user);
        }
      }
    });
  })
);
```

Finally, use the `passort authenticate()` function in the router middleware to attach it to a specific HTTP method-handler function.

In our case, we specify that we don't want to store any authentication details in a session. This is because, when using basic authentication, there is no need to store any user information in a session, as each request contains the `Authorization` header that provides the login details.

Passport's OAuth Strategy

OAuth is an open standard for third party authorization, it defines a delegation protocol used fer authorizing against a third party authentication providers. OAuth uses special tokens, once issued, identify the user instead of user credentials. Let's look closer at OAuth workflow, with a sample scenario. The main actors in the scenario are - a **user** interacting with a **web application,** which consumes a restful service from a **back-end** system providing some kind of data. The web application delegates its authorization to a separate **third-party authorization server.**

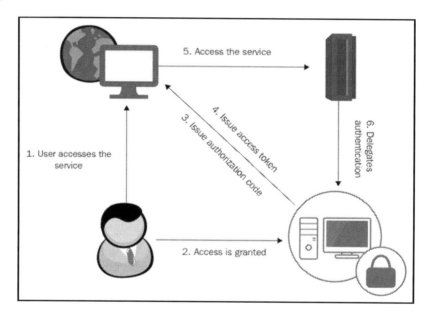

1. The user requests a web application which requires authentication to establish communication with the back-end service. This is the initial request thus the user is still not authenticated, so they get redirected to a login page asking for their credentials for the relevant third party account.

2. After a successful authentication an authorization code is issued by the authentication server to the web application. This authorization code is a composite combination between an issued client-id and a secret issued by the provider. They should be sent from a web application to the authentication server and is exchanged for an access token that has a limited lifetime.

3. The Web application uses the authentication token for authentication until it gets expired. Afterwards it has to request a new token using the authorization code.

Passport.js hides the complexity behind this process with a separate strategy module automating the OAuth workflow. It is available in the npm repository

```
npm install passport-oauth
```

Create an instance of the strategy and supply it with the urls for requesting tokens and for authenticating it together, it is your personal consumer key and a secret phrase of your choice.

```
var passport = require('passport')
  , OAuthStrategy = require('passport-oauth').OAuthStrategy;

passport.use('provider', new OAuthStrategy({
    requestTokenURL: 'https://www.provider.com/oauth/request_token',
    accessTokenURL: 'https://www.provider.com/oauth/access_token',
    userAuthorizationURL: 'https://www.provider.com/oauth/authorize',
    consumerKey: '123-456-789',
    consumerSecret: 'secret'
    callbackURL: 'https://www.example.com/auth/provider/callback'
  }, function(token, tokenSecret, profile, done) {
    //lookup the profile and authenticate   and call done
  }
));
```

Passport.js provides separate strategy wrapping different providers, like linkedin or github. They ensure that your application stays up to date with the token issuing URLs. Once you have made up your mind about the provider you want to support, you should check for specific strategies for them.

Passport's third-party authentication strategies

Today, almost everyone owns at least one personal public social media account, such as Twitter, Facebook, and LinkedIn. Recently, it has become really popular for websites to allow their visitors to authenticate themselves via one of their social accounts by just clicking on an icon to bind their social service account to a service-internal automatically generated account.

This approach is very convenient for web users who are usually permanently logged into at least one of their accounts. If they are not currently logged in, clicking on an icon will redirect them to their social service login page, and, after a successful login, another redirection takes place, ensuring that the user gets the content they originally requested. When it comes to exposing data via a web API, this approach is not really an option.

Publicly exposed APIs cannot predict whether they are to be consumed by a human or by an application. Also, APIs aren't usually consumed directly by humans. Thus, third-party authentication is the only option when you, as API authors, are convinced that the exposed data will be directly available to the end users who have requested it manually through a frontend from an internet browser. Once they have successfully logged into their social account, a unique user identifier will be stored in a session, so your service will need to be able to handle such sessions appropriately.

To enable session support for storing user login information with Passport and Express, you have to initialize the Express session middleware before initializing Passport and its session middleware:

```
app.use(express.session());
app.use(passport.initialize());
app.use(passport.session());
```

Then, specify the user whose details Passport should serialize/deserialize into or out of the session. For that purpose, Passport provides the `serializeUser()` and `deserializeUser()` functions, which store complete user information in a session:

```
passport.serializeUser(function(user, done) { done(null, user); });
passport.deserializeUser(function(obj, done) { done(null, obj); });
```

 The order of initializing the session handling of the Express and Passport middleware is important. The Express session should be passed to the application first and should be followed by the Passport session.

After enabling session support, you have to decide which third-party authentication strategy to rely on. Basically, third-party authentication is enabled via a plugin or application created by the third-party provider, for example, a social service site. We will briefly look at creating a LinkedIn application that allows authentication via the OAuth standard.

Usually, this is done via a pair of public key and a secret (token) associated with the social media application. Creating a LinkedIn application is easy—you just have to log into `http://www.linkedin.com/secure/developer` and fill out a brief application information form. You will be given a secret key and a token to enable the authentication. Perform the following steps to enable LinkedIn authentication:

1. Install the `linkedin-strategy` module—`npm install linkedin-strategy`

2. Get an instance of the LinkedIn strategy and initialize it to the Passport middleware by the `use()` function after session support has been enabled:

```
var passport = require('passport')
  , LinkedInStrategy = require('passport-
  linkedin').Strategy;

  app.use(express.session());
  app.use(passport.initialize());
  app.use(passport.session());

passport.serializeUser(function(user, done) {
  done(null, user);
});

passport.deserializeUser(function(obj, done) {
  done(null, obj);
});

  passport.use(new LinkedInStragety({
    consumerKey: 'api-key',
    consumerSecret: 'secret-key',
    callbackURL: "http://localhost:3000/catalog/v2"
  },
    function(token, tokenSecret, profile, done) {
      process.nextTick(function () {
        return done(null, profile);
      });
    })
  );
```

3. Explicitly specify that the LinkedIn strategy should be used as Passport for each individual route, ensuring that session handling is enabled:

```
router.get('/v2/',
  cache('minutes',1),
  passport.authenticate('linked', { session: true}),
  function(request, response) {
    //...
  }
});
```

4. Provide a means for a user to log out by exposing a logout URI, making use of `request.logout`:

```
router.get('/logout', function(req, res){
request.logout();
  response.redirect('/catalog');
});
```

 The given third-party URLs and service data are subject to change. You should always refer to the service policy when providing third-party authentication.

Authorization

So far, the catalog data service uses basic authentication to protect its routes from unknown users; however, a catalog application should allow only few white-listed users to modify the items inside the catalog. To restrict access to the catalog, we will introduce the concept of authorization, that is, a subset of authenticated users, with appropriate permission allowed.

When Passport's `done()` function is invoked to authenticate a successful login, it takes as an argument a `user` instance of the user that has been granted authentication. The `done()` function adds that user model instance to the `request` object, and, in this way, provides access to it via the `request.user` property, after successful authentication. We will make use of that property to implement a function performing the authorization check after successful authentication:

```
function authorize(user, response) {
   if ((user == null) || (user.role != 'Admin')) {
     response.writeHead(403, { 'Content-Type' :
     'text/plain'});
     response.end('Forbidden');
     return;
   }
}
```

 The HTTP 403 Forbidden status code can be easily confused with 405 Not allowed. However, the 405 Not Allowed status code indicates that a specific HTTP verb is not supported by the requested resource, so it should be used only in that context.

The `authorize()` function will close the `response` stream, returning the `403 Forbidden` status code, which indicates that the logged-in user is recognized but has insufficient permissions. This revokes access to the resource. This function has to be used in each route that carries out data manipulation.

Here's an example of how a `post` route implements authorization:

```
app.post('/v2',
  passport.authenticate('basic', { session: false }),
    function(request, response) {
      authorize(request.user, response);
      if (!response.closed) {
        catalogV2.saveItem(request, response);
      }
    }
);
```

After `authorize()` is invoked, we check whether the `response` object still allows writing to its output by checking the value of the closed property of the `response` object. It will return `true` once the end function of the `response` object has been called, which is exactly what the `authorize()` function does when the user lacks admin permissions. Thus, we can rely on the closed property in our implementation.

Transport layer security

Publicly available information in the web easily becomes the subject of different types of cyber attacks. Often it is not enough just to keep the so-called "bad guys" out. Sometimes, they won't bother gaining authentication at all and may prefer to carry out a **man-in-the-middle (MiM)** attack, pretending to be the final receiver of a message and sniffing the communication channel that transmits the data—or, even worse, altering the data while it flows.

Being a text-based protocol, HTTP transfers data in a human-readable format, which makes it an easy victim of MiM attacks. Unless transferred in an encrypted format, all the catalog data of our service is vulnerable to MiM attacks. In this section, we will switch our transport from an insecure HTTP protocol to the secure HTTPS protocol.

HTTPS is secured by asymmetric cryptography, also known as **public-key encryption**. It is based on a pair of keys that are mathematically related. The key used for encryption is called **public key**, and the key used for decryption is called **private key**. The idea is to freely provide the encryption key to partners who have to send encrypted messages and to perform decryption with the private key.

A typical public-key encryption communication scenario between two parties, *A* and *B*, will be the following:

1. Party *A* composes a message, encrypts it with Party B's public key, and sends it

2. Party *B* decrypts the message with its own private key and processes it

3. Party *B* composes a response message, encrypts it with Party *A*'s public key, and then sends it

4. Party *A* decrypts the response message with its own private key

Now that we know how public-key encryption works, let's go through a sample of HTTPS client-server communication, as shown in this diagram:

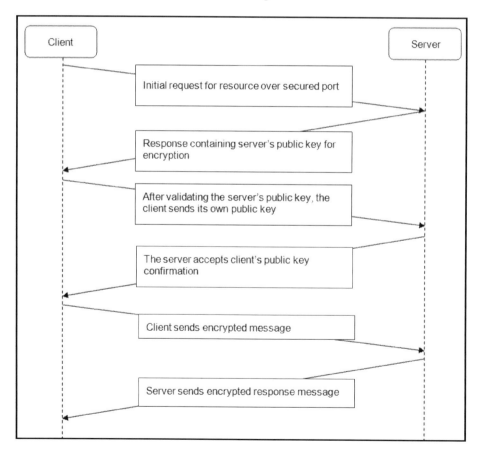

The client sends an initial request against an SSL-secured endpoint. The server responds to that request by sending its public key to be used for encrypting further incoming requests. Then, the client has to check the validity and verify the identity of the received key. After successful verification of the server's public key, the client has to send its own public key back to the server. Finally, after the key exchange procedure is complete, the two parties can start communicating securely.

HTTPS relies on trust; thus, it is vital to have a reliable way of checking whether a specific public key belongs to a specific server. Public keys are exchanged within an X.509 certificate, which has a hierarchical structure. This structure enables clients to check whether a given certificate has been generated from a trusted root certificate. Clients should trust only certificates that have been issued by a known **certificate authority (CA)**.

Before switching our service to use the HTTPS transport, we need a public/private key pair. Since we are not a certificate authority, we will have to use OpenSSL tooling to generate test keys for us.

OpenSSL is available for download at `http://www.openssl.org/`, where source code distributions are available for all popular operating systems. OpenSSL can be installed as follows:

1. Binary distribution is available for download for Windows, and Debian and Ubuntu users can make use of the packaged distribution by executing the following:

   ```
   sudo apt-get install openssl
   ```

    Windows users will have to set an environment variable, OPENSSL_CNF, specifying the location of the `openssl.cnf` configuration file, typically located in the share directory in the installation archive.

2. Now let's generate a test key/value pair with OpenSSL:

   ```
   opensslreq -x509 -nodes -days 365 -newkey rsa:2048-
   keyoutcatalog.pem -out catalog.crt
   ```

OpenSSL will prompt some details required for generating the certificate, such as country code, city, and fully qualified domain name. Afterward, it will generate a private key in the `catalog.pem` file and a public key certificate that will be valid for a year in the `catalog.crt` file. We will be using these newly generated files, so copy them into a new subdirectory, called `ssl`, in the catalog data service directory.

Now we have everything needed to modify our service to use HTTPS:

1. First, we need to switch and use the HTTPS module instead of HTTP and specify the port that we want to use to enable HTTPS communication:

```
var https = require('https');
var app = express();
app.set('port', process.env.PORT || 3443);
```

2. Then, we have to read the private key from the catalog.cem file and the certificate from catalog.crt into an array:

```
var options = {key : fs.readFileSync('./ssl/catalog.pem'),
              cert : fs.readFileSync('./ssl/catalog.crt')
};
```

3. Finally, we pass the array containing the key pair to the HTTPS instance when creating the server and start listening through the specified port:

```
https.createServer(options, app).listen(app.get('port'));
```

That's all you need to do to enable HTTPS for an Express-based application. Save your changes and give it a try by requesting https://localhost:3443/catalog/v2 in a browser. You will be shown a warning message informing you that the server you are connecting to is using a certificate that is not issued by a trusted certificate authority. That's normal, as we generated the certificate on our own, and we are not a CA for sure, so just ignore that warning.

 Before deploying a service on a production environment, you should always ensure that you use a server certificate issued by a trusted CA.

Self-test questions

Go through the following questions:

- Is HTTP basic authentication secure against man-in-the-middle attacks?

- What are the benefits of Transport Layer Security?

Summary

In this chapter, you learned how to protect exposed data by enabling a means of authentication and authorization. This is a critical aspect of any publicly available data service. In addition, you learned how to prevent man-in-the-middle attacks using the secured layer transport protocol between a service and its users. As a developer of such services, you should always consider the most appropriate security features that your application should support.

I hope this was a useful experience! You gained enough knowledge and practical experience, which should have made you much more confident in understanding how RESTful APIs work and how they are designed and developed. I strongly encourage you to go through the code evolution chapter by chapter. You should be able to further refactor it, adopting it to your own coding style. Of course, some parts of it can be further optimized, as they repeat quite often. That is an intentional decision rather than good practice, as I wanted to emphasize their importance. You should always strive to improve your code-base, making it easier to maintain.

Finally, I would like to encourage you to always follow the development of the `Node.js` modules you use in your applications. Node.js has an extraordinary community that is eager to grow rapidly. There is always something exciting going on there, so ensure that you don't miss it. Good luck!

Other Books You May Enjoy

If you enjoyed this book, you may be interested in these other books by Packt:

Mastering Node.js - Second Edition

Sandro Pasquali, Kevin Faaborg

ISBN: 978-1-78588-896-0

- Build an Electron desktop app using Node that manages a filesystem
- Explore Streams and understand how they apply to building networked services
- Develop and deploy an SMS-driven customer service application
- Use WebSockets for rapid bi-directional communication
- Construct serverless applications with Amazon Lambda
- Test and debug with headless browsers, CPU profiling, Mocha, Sinon, and more
- Scale applications vertically and horizontally across multiple cores and web services

Learning Node.js Development

Andrew Mead

ISBN: 978-1-78839-554-0

- Learn the fundamentals of Node
- Build apps that respond to user input
- Master working with servers
- Learn how to test and debug applications
- Deploy and update your apps in the real world
- Create responsive asynchronous web applications

Leave a review - let other readers know what you think

Please share your thoughts on this book with others by leaving a review on the site that you bought it from. If you purchased the book from Amazon, please leave us an honest review on this book's Amazon page. This is vital so that other potential readers can see and use your unbiased opinion to make purchasing decisions, we can understand what our customers think about our products, and our authors can see your feedback on the title that they have worked with Packt to create. It will only take a few minutes of your time, but is valuable to other potential customers, our authors, and Packt. Thank you!

Index

Printed in Poland
by Amazon Fulfillment
Poland Sp. z o.o., Wrocław